Protest in Literature

Dalits, Women and Other Subalterns

Protest in Literature

Dalits, Women and Other Subalterns

Edited by

R.K. Dhawan

Prestige Books International

New Delhi

Published by
Prestige Books International
New Delhi 110 058
prestigebooks@gmail.com
Phone: 9818755529

Associate Offices
50, Clapham Common Westside
London SW 49 A S, U.K.

P.O. Box 2250
Sydney 2001, Australia

ISBN: 978-93-82186-95-3

Printed in India

Contents

Introduction:
Talking about Subaltern Literature

R.K. DHAWAN
University of Delhi

Protest literature constitutes an important segment of contemporary literature. Most of the protest literature in India is based on the following themes:

Economic Exploitation
Subjugation of Women
Fight against Patriarchy
Socio-Political Revolt
Caste and Class War
Crusade against Injustice
Marginalization of the Diaspora
Quest for Identity

The subjects in this arena can vary but often include poverty, discrimination on the basis of caste and class, slavery, violence against women and unfair distribution of wealth between the rich and the poor. The early African-American, for example, had few means to voice their protests and protect their rights, but managed to produce pamphlets to disseminate their ideas. These early protest writings had significant influence on writers who followed, including contemporary novelists Toni Morrison, Alice Walker who have come out with strong and vehement protest in their writings against race, gender and class discrimination.

The phenomenon of protest is nothing new in India. Immense social and cultural movements characterized the nineteenth and early twentieth century. Western education and the

British rule stirred a new awakening. Many writers took up the cause of society and instilled nationalist feelings against the British Raj. The All-India Progressive Writers' Association in the 1930s influenced the Indian novelists to portray life in rural India in the hope of awakening the toiling masses, the economically exploited who find it difficult to make both ends meet. The social criticism of the writers springs from an acute sensitiveness to the disparity between ideals and practices.

The socio-cultural and religious coercive forces in the Indian context have persuaded the marginalized voices to produce literature of resistance. The struggle initiated by B.R. Ambedkar, Jyotiba Phule and Namdeo Dhasal and strengthened by Baburao Bagul, Om Prakash Valmiki, Kancha Ilaiah and Faustina Bama, has led to the institutionalization of Dalit literature and its incorporation in the canon. These writers have succeeded in the portrayal of the lived reality from an insider's perspective. They not only face the politics of resistance from the centre to remain at the fringes but also the politics of assertion from the margins to shift from their defined peripheral space. Thus, "Dalit" meaning 'crushed,' 'ground' or 'broken to pieces' faces the challenge of writing as a political act of emancipation of the Dalit self and the community as a whole. As Raj Kumar has put it, "the Dalits are trying to write themselves into the Indian narrative." (http://timesofindia.indiatimes.com/home/sunday-times/deep-focus/Dalit-literature-goes-global/article show/ 46810541.cms)

Before one introduces the 'theme of protest,' it is imperative to comprehend the historical and literal import of the word 'subaltern.' What is subaltern? How do we define a subaltern? The exact meaning of the term is a bit controversial. Originally, the term 'subaltern' was used in the military for denoting hierarchy in army forces. It was used for subordinates and junior officers, who had no say in decision-making matters. In a way, they were non-entities. In non-military sense, the term 'subaltern' was used first time by the Italian writer Antonio Gramsci (1881-1937) in an essay, in the early 20th century. For him, the term stood for any person or a group of persons, of inferior rank and station, because of race, class, gender, sex, ethnicity or religion.

In the mid-20th century, the term 'subaltern' began to be used as a reference to the colonized people in the South-African subcontinent. In the early 1980s, the term gained a momentum, when at Oxford, Subaltern Studies Group (SSG) was formed under the leadership of Ranajit Guha. It was a group of South Asian scholars, who were interested in the postcolonial and post-imperial societies in South Asia in particular and the developing world in general. In the recent decades, it is regularly used as a term in history, anthropology, sociology and literature.

Historically and politically, subaltern literature is the outcome of European Imperialism. It was mostly in the 19th century when European countries, especially Britain, tried consolidating the imperial power. In the garb of development, Europeans exploited the natives and indigenous people of occupied lands. The process involved military conflict, the massive displacement of the people and greed for profit. But more than accumulation of wealth, it entailed ideological notions of 'subject races,' 'subordinate people and justified the necessity of imposing authority on those, seen as inferior. This was a period in which economic supremacy and political authority of Europe became global.

By 1815, Britain had established itself as a dominant power in the world, as the leader of industrialization and expansion. The time of Queen Victoria's reign, from 1837 to 1901, represented the great age of colonization. It was a time, when there was a wide expansion of the British Empire and the spreading of imperial ideas. Britain, it was believed, had a duty and destiny to rule the world. They were backed by industrial and military power. A special feature of this ideology was their strong belief, that European science, politics and religion were superior to any other. Hence emerged the belief, that reality should be interpreted in these terms.

Along with the belief in Eurocentrism, they also believed that colonized people were lesser human beings—less human, less civilized, and less cultured, more like savages. European anthropologists considered colonized people as primitive, barbarian, inferior, unfit to rule or manage their resources. So, it was the Whiteman's burden to civilize and educate them.

Many women writers have revolted against the eternal female suffering and male dominance. These writers share with their readers the vision of their times—the emancipation of women—and act as social critics and reveal to us what is wrong with the present system and how it can be changed. Revolt is a means by which they instigate a conflict between the old society to which they are attached by class and tradition and the society they would like to create for ideal living. For this, they strongly fight for woman's cause so that her sufferings come to an end. In the fiction of Anita Desai, Chitra Banerjee Divakaruni and Namita Gokhale, we find the emergence of the 'new woman.' Dalit feminist discourse incorporates writings of women, who have voiced their protest against the oppressive power structures operative in the Indian caste, class and patriarchal system. In an attempt to subvert the phallocentric domination in society, as well as in literature, women writers, such as Bama and Baby Kamble, have penned down their painful experience of being female subalterns.

Subaltern literature, thus, articulates the unsaid and unheard ordeal of the marginalized. Unlike Dalit men, only a few Dalit women have written their personal narratives that still remain nameless and faceless in the so-called mainstream literary circles. A major handicap for Dalit women is their lack of education and the ensuing inability to pen down their experiences. The number of literate among Dalits is abysmally low. Majority of these women lead simple and ordinary lives, busy earning their livelihood. They work very hard to survive, as they are much below the poverty line. Despite these challenges, some Dalit women have been able to narrate their sorrows and pains.

It is mainly education and ushering of democracy that brought slow transformation in society. It awakened all sections of society—Dalits, Adivasis and nomadic tribes were no exception. The period from 1920 to 1956 was vastly influenced by Dr. B.R. Ambedkar. This period is often called the Renaissance phase in the history of the Dalit movement. Ambedkar founded Siddhartha College in Mumbai in 1946 and Milind College in Aurangabad in 1947. These colleges acted as catalysts that promoted the young generation to express their sentiments in writing. The Dalits consolidated themselves and held the first conference of Dalit writers in the auditorium of Bengali High School, Dadar, on 2 March 1958. At this conference, a resolution was passed to announce the entry of Dalit literature as a perfect segment of knowledge. Further, it was argued that only Dalits had the experience and authority to narrate the pain of Dalits.

Further, it was argued that only Dalits had the experience and authority to narrate the pain of Dalits. Though Mulk Raj Anand has been generally hailed as the writer of the suffering humanity and a strong advocate of the cause of the poor, yet he was not accepted by Dalits as their representative, because he belonged to a higher caste. Personal experience was said to be the basis of true Dalit writing.

Dalit literature has many affinities with African-American literature. Both these literatures are the outcome of movements for human rights and against exploitation. The most popular form of writing for Dalit and other subaltern writers is the autobiography. Exprcssion of self is the most important feature of a work of art. Autobiography is the mirror in which the writer reflects his own image. However, man's image in the mirror is visible, not only to himself, but also to the people around him. This is what establishes the relationship between self and society.

Alice Walker is one of the most admired African American feminist writers. She is best known for her novel *The Color Purple*, published in 1982. It is an epistolary novel, made up of letters written by Celie. Celie is s fourteen-year-old vulnerable girl, who addresses her letters to 'Dear God.' She has three children by her father. She fights her way to life and questions everything she has been taught. Living in Chicago, Celie spreads her wings. She opens up her own tailor shop and learns to make pants both for women and men. Although the novel is mainly about Celie and her life, it highlights the journeys of the other women, who are in her life, including Shug, Nettie, and Sophia. Together, these women help one another to discover beauty and identity in themselves. Feeling inspired by each other, they muster strength to overcome their oppressive men and emancipate themselves from their clutches. Like Alice Walker, Bama too exhorts the underprivileged women to fight back and not accept humiliation lying down.

Like Bama, Sivakami and Baby Kamble, Aboriginal writers too have been fighting for their rights. *My Place* is an autobiography written by Australian author Sally Morgan. Written in 1987, it is about Morgan's quest for knowledge of her own family's past. The story relates to a young girl growing up to false heritage and not knowing where she is from. The narrative revolves around Morgan's own hometown Perth, Western Australia. Morgan travels to her grandmother's birthplace, exploring a search for her family. She discovers her indigenous Australian heritage—information that was kept secret so far because of the social stigma. Morgan is an Aboriginal ambassador who wants indigenous Australia to feel pride in their identity rather than shame. Like Morgan, Dalit feminist Bama, has in her novels, attempted to articulate and record her experiences of hurt, humiliation and historical neglect by the elite over centuries. Using the "discourse of participation," and drawing from a narrative that speaks about ordinary lives, the Dalit texts convey the voices of women who are on the margins in society.

In the history of mankind, we find that man has always been going out of bounds of the immediate social group he belonged to, and has social, economic or literary exchange with people belonging to other communities. This is because there is a marked distinction between different ethnic entities, often leading to culture-clash. A study of Uma Parameswaran's work reflects the ongoing involvement of immigrant writer with reality. Her first story "The Door Shut behind Me" reflects the sense of wonder and the fear of the immigrant at the new world around him. The writer's second important work *Trishanku* is a sequence of poems covering twenty years. Basing the poem on Indian mythology, she compares the plight of immigrant to Trishanku who is hung in the sky, neither here nor there.

Life in the adopted land places the immigrants in an uncomfortable condition. They are over-awed by the vastness of the new landscape and baffled by the new cultural surroundings. Added to these is racial discrimination. They cry out in anguish:

> It will not be easy, some said,
> And it has not, as we all know
> Who have worked hard, or worse still,
> Have no work at all. (Uma Parameswaran)

Again, the chorus in Uma Parameswaran's play *Dear Didi, My Sister* tells us:

> What we were not told, never guessed,
> Is written on our children's faces.
> Furrowed with tears because of our race
> Or colour.

It is an accepted and acknowledged fact of the literary history of North America that 'Immigrant Writing' or 'Diasporic Writing' has emerged as a distinct and well-identifiable category. There is a strong protest against the 'host' people and their policies.

In the recent years, many writers have espoused the cause of the same-sex relationship. They vehemently protest against the traditional thinking that homosexuality is sinful and desirable. Queer literature which took birth in the West in the twentieth century subsequently manifested in India. India has witnessed in the recent years the emergence of a gay and lesbian movement which has exacerbated state-sponsored social violence against lesbians and gays. One may not agree with the view that homosexuality is external to Indian culture and society. The popular myth that same-sex desire was imported to India by invading West Asian Muslims or colonizing Europeans has been overstated by the so-called nationalists. We have indigenous texts, concepts and traditions which revered and even celebrated sexual ambiguity, in the *Kamasutra*, through sexual dualism, in mysticism, or in female kingdoms. While this is true, orthodox Indians in the present-day India are for maintaining 'family values' and hence their strong opposition to same sex love.

Psychologists categorize all human beings into three groups, based on the predominance of sexual tendencies: heterosexuals, bisexuals and homosexuals. The heterosexuals are those people who establish normal sexual relationship with the members of the opposite sex; the bisexuals are the ones who are erotically interested in both the sexes, whereas the homosexuals are inclined more towards the members of their own sex than towards those of the other. According to Havelock Ellis, most of the human beings possess all these three tendencies in different degrees and therefore develop homosexual inclination at some stage or the other in their life, though the urge may not be strong enough in many people to manifest itself in practice. Some might indulge in homosexuality due to forced separation from the opposite sex and such victims resume normal heterosexual life when brought back to the heterosexual partner. Among those who may rightly be called homosexuals, the urge may be either latent or overt. Latent homosexuals express their inverted sex impulse in their manners and attitude, whereas the overt members give vent to their impulse by choosing members of their own sex and gratifying themselves erotically. With these overt homosexuals, their perversion remains mostly permanent and unchanging and they subsequently grow immune to the emotional and sexual allurements from the opposite sex. Thus, for Havelock Ellis, the conservative psychologist, homosexuality is a perversion and an unnatural behaviour. Joan Blackwood, a lesbian sociologist, argues: "Though it has long been recognized that there is no particular connection between 'morality' and 'naturalness' many critics persist in believing that 'whatever is unnatural is immoral.'" (151)

Many of the 'protest' writings are outcome of economic disparity or culture-clash. *The White Tiger* was prompted by the author's shocked sensibility as he witnessed poverty and corruption in various sectors while working as a reporter. Adiga needs to be credited for his sincere attempt to expose the loopholes in the democratic Indian system in India which, he feels, may be removed through social awareness. The novel is an excellent blend of the two worlds—the rural and the modern. On the other hand, Kiran Desai's Booker Prize winning novel *The Inheritance of Loss* makes a brilliant study of Indian culture—the culture in its transitional phase. It deals with the study of loss—loss of culture, identity, human values, peace and harmony.

Culture-contrast is one of the significant factors of revolt amongst writers. The writers seem deeply involved in values and experiences which are steeped deep in the cultural ethos of India. Rama Mehta in her Sahitya Akademi award-winning novel *Inside the Haveli* espouses Indian culture and values as against the western mode of life.

The advent of Indian Independence brought about a new awareness amongst creative writers. They realized that independence from the British rule would be meaningless without attaining social and economic independence. In the post-

Independence scenario, nationalism became the hallmark of the fiction. More than that, the writers advocated modernism as against orthodoxy and tradition. Many writers discarded the irrational and superstitious practices. They believed in the altruistic aspects of humanism and glorified rational approach in the reformation and reconstitution of humanity at large.

A survey of recent Indian literature reveals that protest is the most dominant theme and it is written with avowed social purpose. It reveals a sweeping revolt against economic exploitation, subjugation of women and suppression of dalits. The plight of the children is no better; they are reducing to begging or selling cheap stuff on the roads. There is a great need for these helpless children to get good education and a better future. Protest literature acknowledges the aspirations of marginalized people in their pursuit of equal rights, freedom of expression, liberty and fraternity.

Aravind Adiga's *The White Tiger* and the "Good Life"

ROBERT (BOB) EASTON
Country Managing Director, Accenture, ANZ

> We are not studying in order to know what virtue is, but to become good for otherwise there would be no profit in it . . . good has rightly been defined as the object of all endeavour.
>
> Aristotle, *Nicomachean Ethics*, cited Melchert 188

The impact of social forces and culture at the societal and organizational level on ethical and moral behaviour has been explored by many philosophers, scholars and novelists over the years (Bazerman & Tenbrunsel; LaFollette; Treviño, den Nieuwenboer & KishGephart). LaFollette, for example wrote, "culture shapes how we eat and talk, what we read and believe, and how we think" (79). Aravind Adiga's *The White Tiger* (2008) has both a plot and a tapestry of themes which draws the reader into reflection on the issue of moral and ethical behaviour in contexts of both social and cultural conditions. The book is a narration of the life of Balram Halwai who, over time, chooses to cheat, steal, lie, forsake his family and ultimately commit murder to escape to a better life. While *The White Tiger* has many stories woven through it, this essay explores virtue versus hedonism as the pathway to the good life and argues that hedonism, which sees life as the sum of net pleasures, is a delusion, rather, the good life which is a life of virtue and is one that ends well.

Since publication of this novel a range of ethical themes have been explored by reviewers in the context of conditions in

India, with some scholars and commentators making comparisons to other nations including the US (for example: Justthinking; Mandelstamm; Narasiman & Chawdhry; Sebastian; Sharma; Waller). An overriding theme in the reviews of the novel is that when corruption is tolerated it becomes rampant and ripples through society and its institutions. When this happens morality becomes ambiguous, and individualism, selfishness and separateness from the collective arise and immoral acts are overlooked. We stop caring about others and move from a 'we' to 'me' centric perspective. This is a world from an ontological view where we become separate from the whole, and our moral decision-making considers only our own happiness versus taking decisions that promote the greatest happiness for the greatest number. This is the world of Balram Halwai, and it could equally be the world of individuals in society and its institutions beyond India who daily are faced with choices to seek pleasure or virtue. Indeed *The White Tiger* skillfully forces readers to contemplate Balram's decision-making and actions to seek *happiness* through individual pleasure or hedonism versus virtue.

The life of Balram Halwai raises a plethora of questions on what is moral and ethical behaviour in search of happiness or the good life in conditions of system-wide corruption, poverty, servitude, exploitation, injustice, inequality, globalization, complex religious belief systems, and an ancient discriminatory caste system. A *consequentialist* perspective might lead one to a conclusion that ends justify means. Balram's moral decision-making and actions justified the ends of escaping his harsh conditions and creating a better life for himself, rather than a better life for the greater good. From a *Relativist* philosophy one might contemplate Balram's actions to cheat, steal, murder, and ultimately sow the seeds of destruction of his family, as being relative to the individual and culture (LaFollette).

The *virtue* ethicists also recognize the challenge of culture. In his writings, Aristotle, suggested that development of morality or of virtue, occurs not through reading a treatise on virtue but through witnessing the virtue and morality in others (or immorality and unethical behaviour), and through patterning and mentoring and then through disposition and habit formation (Gini; Melchert). However while Aristotle and the other great sages would recognize that social conditions, culture of corruption and negative role models confronting Balram daily, create moral ambiguity for him, in the end ethics involves the free will to make choices and to choose what is good and right versus what is pleasurable:

> The point is that moral virtue is concerned with pleasures and pain. We do bad actions because of the pleasure going with them, and abstain from good actions because they are hard and painful. Therefore, there should be some direction from an early age, as Plato says, with a view to taking pleasure in, and being pained by, the right things. (Melchert 192)

From the perspective of virtue ethics, therefore, Balram's ethical and moral choices, while influenced by social forces and culture, are determined by the bad moral decision-making which then becomes habitual and pleasure seeking. Herein lies a lesson for all of us, while it is easy to blame social forces and culture, in the end as humans we have a choice and there is sufficient evidence in the novel *The White Tiger* that Balram was exposed to examples of virtue and to what is right and wrong. For example, throughout Balram's personal narration in *The White Tiger*, we see glimpses of empathy and sympathy and many examples where Balram is aware of, and has therefore learned about, right from wrong; moral versus immoral behaviour. He uses the word virtue in describing Mr. Ashok (193) and he is aware of the consequences of his hedonic choices. For example he notes: ". . . only a man who is prepared to see his family destroyed—hunted, beaten, and burned alive by the masters—can break out of the coop. That would take no normal human being, but a freak, a pervert of nature. It would, in fact, take a White Tiger" (150). We also see recognition that murder is wrong but no guilt because he reasons that the ends justify the means (269).

Throughout the novel Balram does not lose his sense of what is morale, rather, just like the great organizations and leaders in recent memory who have fallen from grace and destroyed their legacies, he chooses to act from a sense of pleasure and ambition versus virtue. When this choice is made, a litany of evil emerges and Balram has succumbed to the belief that happiness or the good life is the summed net pleasures across life, that is, the sum of good moments minus the bad moments. One might argue that the social forces and cultural conditions in India moderate the classical ethical problem of how to live a good life, however in an ironical way the culture itself and the deep tradition of Hinduism provide what others might term a code of conduct, or ethical guide rails for how to live the good life which Balram and those around him choose to relinquish for pleasure.

Within Hinduism there are normative guidelines. Ethics, virtuous behaviour, right morale conduct, the good life are complex concepts, which have been debated over centuries, in both Western and Hindu literature. What appears similar, however, in both western and Hindu traditions, is that morale reasoning and ethics is not something one can impose on an individual, rather it is something one has to strive for without reference to rewards. In Hinduism, virtuous and ethical conduct is something that one chooses to live up to; for Hindus, in this *dharmic* life, ethical choices and the actions that follow are made in pursuit of being the best human: "An ethical life in Hinduism is essential for a liberated life, one without craving . . . and by abstaining from evil" (as cited in Wikipedia). Nishpapananda wrote that "according to Hinduism, the one universal duty of all human beings is the practice of dharma" (1). Nishpapananda equates Dharma to practising virtue.

The Hindu concept of *Dharma*, one might argue is therefore similar to Aristotle's concept of *eudaimonia*, which is concerned with living the most complete good life well, of pursuing virtue and of functioning well, rather than hedonic happiness or merely experiencing pleasure and feeling good (Fowers; LaFollette; Melchert). Like Hinduism, Aristotle tells us that the virtuous life comes from constant striving, or habitual attention to living life well. For Aristotle, the good life cannot be realized in a vacuum away from others, from society. Balram, like all individuals lived in community of others, his moral choices and actions are taken at the expense of others, including his family—and in forsaking his family, which included condemning them to at a minimum of dishonor and potentially death. In doing so he turns his back on virtue in pursuit of pleasure.

Some commentators have described his acts of individualism as revealing his true psychopathic nature, a nature characterized by deceit, impulsiveness, recklessness, and one devoid of caring for others including his own family (Narasiman & Chawdhry; Sebastian). His choices and actions consistently show a disregard for any sense of morality and the coveting of ambition and power as he "goes about heroically planning his heinous crimes" (Sebastian 243). Any sense of future good deeds, for example, establishing a school in Bangalore is purely about pursuit of power and ambition, versus a search for doing good, for repentance. Balram muses, for example: "an English-language school—for poor children in Bangalore. A school where you won't be allowed to corrupt anyone's head with prayers and stories about God or Gandhi—nothing but the facts of life for these kids. A school full of White Tigers, unleashed on Bangalore! We'd have this city at our knees, I tell you. I could become the Boss of Bangalore" (193)

The concept of *eudemonia* has a meaning component to it that goes beyond the summed net pleasures (Rozin & Stellar), researchers have sought to unravel the connection between pleasure and the meaning of the *good life* (Argyle; Daniel Kahneman & Riis; King & Napa; Rozin & Stellar). Kahneman's work supports the thesis that the *good experience* depends almost entirely on how it ends because his research shows that, with respect to our pleasures, our memories will be biased toward the experience at the finale of an experiential event—this is referred to in the literature as *peak-end* theory. This research shows just how powerful endings can be and if we apply this peak-end theory to life, the *good life* is one that ends well because our memories will be biased towards experience in the final years of life. In *Authentic Happiness*, Seligman wrote "In your own life, you should take particular care with endings, for their color will forever tinge you memory" (7).

The *good life* debate spawns an array of vexing questions for contemplation and research. For example, if we hold the *total* amount of pleasure constant, a scary thought for the hedonists, which is a better life: one gradually rising to happiness in life, or one gradually declining? Further, Rozin and Stellar followed a line of inquiry on the *good life* that focused on testing the effect of posthumous events on our perceptions or assessments of the *good life*, that is, whether posthumous events lead us to reevaluate the assessment of the quality of one's life. Across a number of studies, they found that happiness ratings were different for life and posthumous events. Specifically, they found that "posthumous events reflect a judged goodness of a life" (277), and this could be accounted for by either: (1) a belief in life after death thru legacies, or a "halo" effect where the change in ending shifts the quality of life story; or (2) a valence affect from the ending or information brought to life after the event, which could be after death. This valence of ending, or information, leads to retroactive altering or reevaluation of the assessment of the life story or "true" meaning to the event or life. Simply, we alter assessment of the quality of life based on new information that shows the life in a better or worse light.

Rozin and Stellar speculate that the pleasure we experience is not in the here and now, but instead in forms of recollections or anticipation, and the assessment of the quality and meaning of life is not a summed experience of pleasures across a life span; rather the *good life* does depend almost entirely on how it ends. Rozin also posited that the implication of this research is that one does not have to believe in life after death if we believe that an assessment of a *good life* is still negotiable after one is dead—retrospective altering offers us a way to deal with death. Death is one ending but it is not the only way to frame a life. An intriguing thought is that there can be two endings in life, that is, it can be framed at death and then altered post-death.

In the context of endings and meanings, and of *peak-ends*, this story has interesting irony to it that highlights the folly of the hedonist view. Following the murder of Ashok and his rise to the status of a successful Bangalore entrepreneur, Balram feels he has transcended from his lower caste to a higher status, that is, from "the darkness" of his low caste to "light" of a higher social status; he had escaped the "rooster coop." To achieve this however he had to cheat, lie, steal, and murder, all vices versus virtues; moreover he had to condemn his family, a shameful act in both traditional and modern India. The first irony however lies in the fact that to escape the darkness Balram had to forego the morality he learned in "darkness." This is ironical since within Hinduism there is a concept of *Varna* which is a perspective that one's caste is dependent on one's character, and that while birth caste is dominant it is possible to move from the "darkness" to the "light" through developing and demonstrating morale character (Buch).

The second irony lies in making the choices he made to escape the "darkness" and his lower caste, in pursuit of freedom, he violated many of the tenets of Hinduism's perspective on the good life. Hinduism does not deny Balram's hedonist impulses, in fact in Hinduism, one of the four goals of life is *Kama* or pleasure (Buch). However, like Aristotle's version of virtue, Dharma or the practice of virtue is the pathway to the good life and it is through Dharma, that Moksha is achieved which in Hinduism represents "freedom, liberation from all bondages and suffering" (Nishpapananda 2). Hence seeking hedonic pleasure does not bring him in the light but condemns him to eternal darkness and reinforces the notion that the good life is one that ends well. Interestingly, Buch wrote that in Hinduism, virtue is power, "to be weak is miserable, virtue is, after all, virility" (46).

To bring to life the importance of virtue and moral choice even in the conditions Balram faced, it is instructive to contrast the life of Balram Halwai with that of Nelson Mandela. Mandela spent 30+ years in prison, in what many would describe as hell and abject displeasure and great suffering. He was surrounded by many of the cultural and structural norms and social forces confronting Halwai, including: ridicule, racism, corruption, theft, and brutality within society and the institutions of the ruling elite and his own party. He faced similar choices, albeit on a larger scale, to Balram—hedonism, pleasure or virtue. He chose a life of virtue, one of forgiveness and courage, of selflessness and empathy and one of virtuous choices and in doing so established a legacy that is enduring; one we reflect on with awe and respect. We can only imagine the consequences of Mandela making the similar choices to Balram for the nation of South Africa and for the world. Peak-end theory and duration neglect mean that while the sum of the pleasurable experiences may not equal a good life for Mandela himself, the great ending matters much more for the evaluation of his life as *good*; as triumph of virtue over hedonism.

Culture and social forces do impact what is considered moral or ethical, *The White Tiger* highlights the catalytic and transitive forces of a corrupt and unjust culture and of social forces that create ambiguity for moral decision-making. Clearly moral choices and endings are extremely important, they are important in providing meaning to life and they are important in current and retrospective appraisals of the *good life*. While we are left wondering how Balram's life will end, daily the press across the world in different cultures shines the light on people who have chosen hedonism over virtue. Both practical example and research show that the hedonist view is a delusion and that the *good life* is one that ends well. In his treatise *Nicomachean Ethics*, Aristotle's description of the fragility of human existence, bodes a warning to Balram's pursuit of pleasure:

> There are many changes and all kinds of chances through a lifetime, and it is possible for a man who is really flourishing to meet with great disaster in old age, like Priam of Troy. No one gives the name happy to a man who meets with misfortune like that and dies miserably. (Melchert 191)

In conclusion, Balram has discovered that hedonism is a shortcut to happiness, but we know these shortcuts are short lived: history is replete with examples that show there are no shortcuts to the good life. For the good life, endings matter; they mattered for Nelson Mandela, they mattered for many leaders, organizations and cultures brought down from seeking pleasure versus virtue, from bad morale character; they will matter for Balram; and they will matter you and me! Most importantly this all matters for the future of India and its people, as Narasiman and Chawdhry concluded their analysis of *The White Tiger*:

> The novel is an intelligent and ruthless portrait of India in which downtrodden people like Balram suffer under the rich. . . . But the Indian people should not overlook the bloody acts, opportunism, entrepreneurial success of people like Balram and emergence of Socialists in India, and it is the duty of each and every citizen that they should try their level best not to indulge in corruption activities (taking and giving) which may give birth to so many Balrams which is very very dangerous to thc socicty. (9)

Finally—follow hedonism at your peril, striving for virtue is the only escape in the long run from challenges one faces in life, hedonism is a delusion. Yes culture creates ambiguities so one external to a culture or not subject to social forces might struggle to rationalize decisions taken by another, but for a society like India faces with these conditions, the actions and character of people like Balram who take the hedonic route must be derided. The true heroes are those who do not succumb to the seduction of pleasure and of the excuse of culture and social forces. In both the Aristotlean and in some ways the Dharmic sense the good life comes from habitual attention to virtue regardless of what life throws our way.

Bibliography

Adiga, Aravind (2008). *The White Tiger*. New York: Free Press. doi: 10.1176/appi.ajp.2009.09091322

Argyle, M. (1999). "Causes and Correlates of Happiness." In D. Kahneman, E. Diener & N. Schwatz, ed., *The Foundations of Hedonic Psychology* (353-73). New York: Russell Sage.

Bazerman, M.H. & A.E. Tenbrunsel (2011). *Blind Spots: Why we fail to do what's right and what to do about it*. Princeton, NJ: Princeton University Press.

Buch, M. (1921). *The Principles of Hindu Ethics. Ethics*. Baroda: Arya Sudharak Printing Press. doi:10.1086/207792

Fowers, B.J. (2012). "An Aristotelian framework for the human good." *Journal of Theoretical and Philosophical Psychology*, 32 (1), 10-23. doi:10.1037/a0025820

Gini, A. (1997). "Moral leadership and business ethics." *Journal of Leadership & Organizational Studies*, 4 (4), 64-81. doi: 10.1177/107179199700400406

Justthinking. (2011). *The White Tiger* and the Indian culture of corruption. http://cannotstopthethought.blogspot.com/2011/10/white-tiger-and-indian-culture-of.html

Kahneman, D. & J. Riis. (2005). "Living, and thinking about it : two perspectives on life." In N. Baylis, F. Huppert & B. Kaverne, ed., *The Science of Well-Being* (285-304). Oxford: Oxford University Press. doi:10.1126/science.1103572

King, L. & C.K. Napa. (1998). "What makes a life good?" *Journal of*

Personality and Social Psychology, 75 (1), 156-65. http://www.ncbi.nlm.nih.gov/pubmed/9686456

LaFollette, H. (2007). *The Practice of Ethics*. Malden, MA: Blackwell.

Mandelstamm, A. (2011, March 30). *The White Tiger*: Fiction from India, cautionary tale for US. http://www.occasionalplanet.org/2011/03/30/fiction-from-indiacautionary-tale-for-us/

Melchert, N. (2002). "Aristotle: The reality of the world. The good life." In *The great conversation: A Historical Introduction to Philosophy*, 4th edition (186-95). Boston, MA: McGraw Hill. http://scholar.google.com/scholar?hl=en&btnG=Search&q=intitle:Aristotle:+The+reality+o f+the+world.+The+good+life#0

Narasiman, R.R. & V.S. Chawdhry. (2013). "Balram's quest for freedom in Adiga's *The White Tiger*," *The Criterion: An International Journal in English*, IV (V), 1-10.

Nishpapananda, S. (2010). "Hinduism, happiness, and the good life." *Interdisciplinary Journal of the Dedicated Semester. Happiness: Traditions and Tensions*.

Rozin, P. & Stellar, J. (2009). "Posthumous events affect rated quality and happiness of lives," *Judgment and Decision Making*, 4 (4), 273-79. http://journal.sjdm.org

Sebastian, A.J. (2009). "Poor-rich divide in Aravind Adiga's *The White Tiger*," *Journal of Alternative Perspectives in the Social Sciences*, 1 (2), 229-45. http://search.ebscohost.com/login.aspx? direct=true &db=a9h&AN=46815711&site=ehostlive

Seligman, M. (2002). *Authentic happiness: Using the new positive psychology to realize your potential for lasting fulfillment*. New York: Free Press.

Sharma, P. (2013). Book review: *The White Tiger* by Aravind Adiga. http://storiesinmoments.com/2013/07/20/book-review-thewhite-tiger-by-aravind-adiga-winner-of-the-man-booker-prize-2008/

Treviño, L.K., N. den Nieuwenboer & J.J. Kish-Gephart (2014). (Un)ethical behaviour in organizations. *Annual Review of Psychology*, 65, 635-60. doi:10.1146/annurev-psych-113011-143745

Waller, K. (2012). Redefinitions of India and individuality in Adiga's *The White Tiger*. *Comparative Literature and Culture*, 14 (2). doi:/10.7771/1481-4374.1965

Wikipedia. (2015). http://en.wikipedia.org/wiki/The_White_Tiger

A Study of Subaltern in Terms of Class: Aravind Adiga's *The White Tiger*

M. NIRMALA
N.M. Govt. Degree & P.G. College, Jogipet
PARVATI V.
J.N.T.U.H. College of Engineering, Hyderabad

Literally the term "Subaltern" means "of inferior rank." Originally the term was used to denote the lower ranks in British army. Antonio Gramsci, an Italian Marxist was the first person to adopt this term to denote the marginalized sections of the society, which may include peasants, workers and other groups which don't have access to the hegemonic power structure. Later Ranajit Guha, an Indian Marxist historian, used this term in *Subaltern Studies* "as a name for the general attribute of subordination in South Asian society whether this is expressed in terms of class, caste, age, gender and office or in any other way." (vii)

Aravind Adiga's novel *The White Tiger* strongly speaks for the subaltern sections of the society, who are below the poverty line and don't have access to good education or other basic amenities which they are entitled to. Though the novel was criticized as a cynical narrative about India by many critics, it certainly speaks for the subaltern in terms of class. Adiga got inspired to create the character of Balram Halwai, the protagonist, when he met a number of poor people while travelling across India as a journalist. In an interview, he stated: "Many of the Indians I met while I travelled through India blended into Balram. But the character is ultimately of my own invention. I wanted to depict someone from India's underclass which is perhaps 400 million strong and which has rarely missed out on the economic boom and which remains invisible in most films and books coming out of India."

Balram Halwai, a the true representative of subaltern in terms of class, was born into the lowest strata of the society. His education came to an abrupt end due to his poor financial position and he was forced to work as a child labour. The novel speaks about his journey from the class of "have-nots" to that of "haves." The novel gives a detailed picture of the exploitation of the poor by the rich and also speaks about the patriarchal power structures which seek to keep the social order intact. Balram was born in an extremely poor family in a remote village named "Laxmangarh" in the state of Bihar. His father was a rickshaw puller who suffered from tuberculosis and finally succumbed to it due to lack of proper medication.

At the outset, Balram speaks about two Indias, "India of Light" and "India of Darkness," the urban and the rural India respectively. "India of Light" represents the jubilant life of the rich, living in metros with all the luxuries at their doorstep, whereas "India of Darkness" represents the poor working class, leading a wretched life in rural India. They are deprived of the basic human needs and have no access to good education or medication or hygienic living conditions.

Balram's schooling came to an abrupt end with his cousin's marriage, because he had to help the family to repay the loan taken for his cousin's dowry. Then his grandmother joined him as a child labour in a teashop in the nearby town Dhanbad. Balram was a keen observer and all the lessons of life he learnt were through observation. While serving tea and wiping the tables, his eyes and ears were wide open to absorb the powerful lessons. Balram describes: "And it was at the tea shop in this city built by coal wiping a table and lingering to overhear a conversation, that my life changed." (53)

From the conversation of customers, he gathers the information that car drivers are paid good salary, and he makes it his aim from that day to learn driving and to be a driver of a wealthy master. On much pleading, his grandmother concedes to pay the fee for his driving classes and he learns driving with great enthusiasm. The big opportunity comes his way when the wealthy landlord's son Ashok returns from the U.S. along with his wife Pinky madam. They decide to stay in Delhi and appoint Balram as their car driver. It is then that he shifts from Laxmangarh to Delhi, from "India of Darkness" to "India of Light." But there, amidst the glittering streets of New Delhi, he realizes the bitter truth that there is an unfathomable abyss between the privileged and the underprivileged sections of the society and by no possible method can he bridge the gap except by crossing the limit.

The novel proclaims that whatever crime is committed by the poor should not be attributed to them, but to their hunger and poverty. The author focuses on the point that when the basic needs are not fulfilled, the desperation may result in such aggressive acts as Balram's decision to kill his master. After looking at the glitz and glamour of the city, Balram too wants to enjoy the luxurious life and looks around for an option to bridge the gap between the two classes. Desperate frustration leads him to take the abominable decision. His mind is filled with vengeance and bitterness rather than growth and prosperity.

The tone of the novel is mockingly derisive, without any sympathy towards the poor. Balram laughs at the poor working class people for their adherence to hollow and empty morals. Though they have a good chance to steal money from their master, they never do that because their minds have been conditioned with faithfulness towards their master and morality towards life. Balram feels that it is not necessary to uphold these morals because however strongly he may stick to honesty and loyalty, these values will not make him the master. Adiga uses the powerful image of "Rooster coop" to describe this:

> Go to Old Delhi behind the Jama Masjid, and look at the way they keep chickens there in the market. Hundreds of pale hens and brightly coloured roosters, stuffed tightly into wire-mesh cages, packed as tightly as worms in a belly, pecking each other and shitting on each other, jostling just for breathing space; the whole cage giving of a horrible stench—the stench of terrified, feathered flesh. On the wooden desk above this coop sits a grinning young butcher, showing off the flesh and organs of a recently chopped-up chicken, still oleaginous with a coating of dark blood. The roosters in the coop smell the blood from above. They see the organs of their brothers lying around them. They know they're next. Yet they do not rebel. They do not try to get out of the coop. (173)

Adiga's objection is that the servant class serves its masters willingly. They are not ready to come out of the perpetual servitude as their minds have been programmed accordingly. Even when they have an opportunity to come out of that wretchedness, they do not utilize it. Balram was desperate to become a master because he does not find any justification in leading a life of servitude. He is not bothered about the method which he follows for his emancipation. Hence, he took the deliberate decision which helped him to take the gigantic leap from slavery to masterdom. Thus Balram arrogantly declares "in the olden days there were one thousand castes and destinies in India. These days, there are just two castes: Men with big bellies, Men with small bellies. And only two destinies: eat or get eaten up." Balram decides to become a man with big belly.

With all the loopholes in the system, the gross injustice he faced in life and the ill-treatment by his master, he doesn't consider it a crime to kill his master. The author wants to warn the privileged classes of India that the day of revolt is not too far. India cannot become a developed country unless and until the class division gets obliterated from the society. Every human being has the right to lead a free and independent life and none should prevent him from enjoying this privilege. For Adiga, there are three categories of people, the first are landlords and politicians who are in the upper strata of the society, who make the rules and run the show. The second category is that of the upper middle class Indians, well-educated and employed those who take services from the labour class, are also in compliance with the system which allows exploitation of the marginalized sections. Adiga wants to expose the hypocrisy of Indian middle class people who pose as the saviours of their servants.

In metropolitan cities, these two categories, the master class and the servant class co-exist: the master class takes services from the servant class without any hesitation or guilt. They satisfy their conscience with false theories and shallow vanity. They are indifferent to the poor living conditions of the working class.

In comparison, we find that in the advanced countries of America and Europe, human services are highly expensive and even the wealthy are forced to do all the household chores themselves. There is no exploitation of human services in that society. In India, illiteracy, limited employment opportunities for unlimited youth and the corrupt political system are some of the factors which allow the exploitation of the subaltern class:

> Things are different in the Darkness. There, every morning, tens of thousands of young men sit in the tea shops, reading the newspaper, or lie on a charpoy humming a tune, or sit in their rooms talking to a photo of a film actress. They have no job to do today. They know they won't get any job today. They've given up the fight. They're the smart ones.
>
> The stupid ones have gathered in a field in the centre of the town. Every now and then a truck comes by, and all of them pushed me; I pushed back, but the truck scooped up only six or seven men and left the rest of us behind. They men in the field rush to it with their hands outstretched, shouting, "Take me! Take me!"
>
> Everyone was off on some construction or digging job—the lucky bastards. Another half-hour of waiting. Another truck came. Another scramble, another fight. After the fifth or sixth fight of the

> day, I finally found myself at the head of the crowd, face to face with the truck driver. (54-55)

Adiga ruthlessly exposes the bitter facts about India's corrupt political system, lack of employment opportunities for youth, laziness and lethargy they are steeped in. All these factors reflect a bad picture of India. But Adiga says: "At a time when India is going through great changes and, with China, is likely to inherit the world from the west, it is important that writers like me try to highlight the brutal injustices of society." Adiga expects the educated middleclass Indians to support and help him in fulfilling this herculean task, with constructive action plan rather than with hypocritical philosophy.

The novel is not named after the protagonist Balram Halwai, but after a unique creature in the universe, namely "The White Tiger." Balram was not an individual but representative of the underprivileged sections of the society. Throughout the novel, Adiga focuses on the unbridgeable gap between the rich and the poor. In the over-populated Delhi, the rich and the poor co-exist harmoniously. The rich lead a life of luxury with 24-hour water facility and electricity, take the services from maids, cooks and car drivers, who without the slightest grudge serve their masters and mistresses with utmost loyalty. This servant class people live beside the luxuriously illuminated malls and multiplexes. Their living conditions are pathetic, without proper sanitation or drainage system. With no privacy or decency, they defecate openly and live under the bridges or on the road side. In one word, they live in sub-human conditions. Karuna Kara Roul says: "Karl Marx demarcated two classes in the existing society: haves and have-nots or bourgeois and proletariats—exploitive and exploited. Adiga says it: men with big bellies and men with small bellies—the rich and the poor. Politically it may be ruler and ruled."

While speaking about the Indian English literature and its purpose of cleansing the society, to bring the attention of the readers onto the social evils prevalent in the society and thereby to initiate a change in the mindset of the people, Indian English literature has played an important role till now. In the words of Tanushree Singh "one of the most important social issues it has been dealing with through the decades in the class structure in India." Indian society has for centuries been rigidly hierarchical with the burden of socio-economic class disparities being further aggravated by caste distinctions (a term that includes both 'varna' and 'jati') observed not just by Hindus but also by several non-Hindu communities. Mulk Raj Anand among the earlier Indian English novelists is best known for his treatment of this subject, in novels like *Coolie* and *Untouchable*. Adiga also stands beside him with this novel.

Adiga, through various incidents, reveals the apathy and the indifference with which the rich treat the poor and he wants the privileged class to realize the fact that this cannot continue forever. The rich cannot take the poor for granted all the time. This indifference may lead to dangerous consequences. Obviously the novel gives a clarion call to the people of the nation to bring about the required change in their mindset and to pave the way for the establishment of an egalitarian society, where each human being has his own space, and lives with dignity and self respect.

Bibliography

Adiga, Aravind. *The White Tiger*, Harper Collins, New Delhi, 2009

Interview, 16 October 2008, http://www.rediff.com/news/2008/oct/16adiga.htm>

Guha, Ranajit (1982) *Subaltern Studies I: Writings on South Asian history and society*. Oxford University Press, New Delhi.

Singh, Tanushree "Class Structure in A. Roy's *The God of Small Things* and Aravind Adiga's *The White Tiger*," *Aravind Adiga's The White Tiger, A Symposium of Critical Response*, ed. R.K. Dhawan, 113-21, Prestige, New Delhi.

Roul, Karuna Kara. "Class and Cultural Consciousness: A Perspective on *The White Tiger*," *Ibid*.

Violence against Sex Workers in Indian Society

BOLLA MADHAVI
Osmania University, Hyderabad

My paper focuses on the atrocities experienced by the sex workers in India. Social alienation and wrongful treatment of sex workers have been studied through *The Autobiography of a Sex Worker* by Nalini Jameela. Very courageous and outspoken writer Nalini Jameela, a sex worker and a social activist, was born in a low caste family in Kerala. A school dropout, she worked as a child labour to support her family. She entered into the profession of sex work at the age of 24. Her autobiography deals with the real life experiences of a common Indian woman who chose prostitution as a source of her livelihood.

The book became controversial as well as bestseller; it was first published in Malayalam and later translated into English. Nalini is the narrator of this story; her schooling stopped at the age of nine and she joined as a labour in a clay mine with long working hours. Later she became an ayah in a lawyer's house to look after children; there she was abused by Ittamash (Balettan's sister's husband). Nalini says about this incident: "Everyone said that it was a terrible mistake to have gone alone into Ittamash's room" (15). Now all the family members found fault with Nalini, not Ittamash and finally she accepted it as her fault. This is how our society tries to silence the abused children.

Nalini started sex work to support her children after her husband's death. She writes about her first client and the harassment by police: "The same handsome man handed me over to the police in the morning. Men can be both tender and cruel at the same time. I learned that lesson from my very first client." At daybreak, the police jeep came again to pick us up. We were dropped at the Mission Quarters near the town. Just as I started walking away, another police jeep halted near me. Two policemen got out and barked rudely: "Get Inside."

This was during the Emergency when sudden arrests were common. As soon as we got to the police station, the caning started. We were caned on the soles of our feet. In my anger and distress at this treatment, I shouted, "Police to sleep with by night; police to give a thrashing by day." In between beatings, the Assistant Station Inspector jeered, "So what did you think? That if you slept with 'saar' at night. From this I understood that my dream-man was higher up than all of these officers.' Police conduct raids and this vulnerable section is tortured; they accept this exploitation because they have no other option: "Some time later, the Sub-Inspector came in. He was kind to me, he told them to stop beating me. Come with me for the night, and you will be let off. I accepted it and saved my neck." (26). Police extort money from the sex workers, If they fail to pay money these powerful policemen ask for sexual pleasures in return.

Most of the sex workers experienced great violence from their clients, brokers, family members and society. These isolated women were forced by the society to accept themselves as suppressed women. Heart-rending story of a sex worker has been reported by the Jaago Re team here; a sex worker says: "One night, after making a deal with my client we were at his place, I noticed that there was a bunch of four other men there, all drunk out of their minds. I had started to protest but by then it was too late, I was physically beaten and gangraped by five of them despite telling them that I had HIV. They taunted me saying that, I was lying and in a hurry to go between my legs'.' Sex workers are sure to experience higher levels of violence at their working place. Unknowingly, she married an HIV infected person at the age of 15, had two sons and later she chose this profession to support her two children. Lack of education is one of the major causes that lead to stigmatization of sex worker. She again uncovered the harsh attitude of the police: "I escaped by hiding myself in a truck and went to the nearest police station. I had shown the bruises I had on my body and private parts, and asked for help. Their reaction was, you are a sex worker, how does this classify as rape when you are whoring around town for money?" The police didn't consider her rape as violence. They refused to register her case.

Gangrape, child abuse, gender inequality, child marriages and dowry deaths are some of the social evils deeply rooted in Indian community. Sex workers are not accepted. In *The Autobiography of a Sex Worker*, Nalini shows that our society won't allow them to live their lives with dignity. Nalini's mother-in-law demanded more money and accepted her earnings but Nalini couldn't go to her home. Later Nalini married Koyakka; it was said that he had married twice and had divorced both his wives but it was half-truth, his second wife had gone for delivery. Society accepts a man with two wives. Nalini said about Koyakka's brother-in-law, "They had all heard by then, that I had been a sex worker. This seemed convenient; his brother-in-law started inviting me to bed" (48). Nalini's experience clearly shows that our heinous society rejects the marginalized sex workers who escape from that evil trap and look for social acceptance.

Sometimes, children are also victims of ill-treatment in their society. Zeenath, a girl child was born to Nalini and Kayakka. He took care of other things but was not ready to own his daughter. Nalini said: "I realized his intention, when he made a bad joke once. When Koyakka was taking Nasrat (child by his other wife) to show his mother, I asked him to take my daughter along too. He replied, I'll abandon your girl on the train. The kid born *harrat* (in faith) must be cared for, but not the kid born *haraam* (outside faith)" (48).When Nalini learnt that Koyakka had refused to recognize their child, she decided to divorce him. Children of sex workers also face discrimination in society. As a mother, Nalini struggles to protect her daughter from the world of sex work.

Miserable conditions of socially isolated child of a sex worker are beautifully explored by the postcolonial woman writer Kamala Markandaya in her famous work *Nectar in a Sieve*. Rukmani is the protagonist of this novel and her daughter Irawaddy is a helpless woman abandoned by her husband, claiming that she is a barren women. Irawaddy, innocent and obedient girl finally turns into a prostitute. Ira entered into this profession to save her younger brother's life. Rukmani said: "The lips of her wounds had hardly drawn together when Ira was on her feet again. Where do you go? I said to her. Rest a little longer; the marks are still livid." "Rest," she said contemptuously. "How can I rest or any one rest? Can you not hear the child?" (102) Rukmani understood the reason behind Kuti's improvement—it was Ira who was feeding him and not her prayers.

Ira's son Sacrabani was a socially isolated child; other children never played with him. Rukmani says once, "Poor child, he had to suffer the behaviour of his elders" (129). Sacrabani had so many questions in his mind. Once he asked Ira:

> "Mother, what is a bastard"? Ira was searching for proper answer.
> "Why do you ask?"
> "I want to know?"
> "It is a child whose birth his mother did not wish for."
> "Oh," he said, looking at her speculatively."Did you wish me to be born?"
> "Yes, of course, darling," Ira cried (129).

Sacrabani was called a bastard. He was humiliated just because he was born to a sinful woman.

No one is born a prostitute; situations force them to sell their bodies. Their circumstances compel them to choose this highly risky profession against their will. "We aren't the only people to commit this crime. There are lawyers who come to us; there are doctors and businessmen. It isn't fair that all of them are considered respectable and we alone are made into criminals." (Nalini Jameela's First Public Speech 87). It is ironical that sex workers are treated as immoral women, their clients are considered dignified men. Men should also be arrested along with the sex workers. In India, every individual has right to freedom, right to live with dignity. Victims of sexual violence accept everyday torture by their clients. They believe strongly, that it's very common to be raped by so many men; they consider themselves as voiceless creatures. So, restoring their dignity is necessary. Society should change its attitude towards these suppressed women. Nalini Jameela demanded stopping of the police harassment. Government of India should introduce some Policies for them and those should be implemented intensively.

Bibliography

Jameela, Nalini. *The Autobiography of a Sex Worker*. Navi Mumbai, Repro India, 2005.

Markandaya, Kamala. *Nectar in a Sieve*. New Delhi: Penguin, 1982.

www.jaagore.com/current-issues/you-are-a-sex-worker-how-can-you-be-raped.

From Margins to Mainstream: Some Perspectives on Women Empowerment in Indian Women Fiction

P. VIJAYALAXMI
Govt. Degree & P.G. College for Women, Nalgonda

One of the major aspects of women empowerment in India is to change the attitude of society towards women. The problem in India is that the society never worked on the premise of gender equality since a long time. Atrocities and discrimination against women is a way of daily life. There is an attitude which prevails in India where women are considered to be worthwhile of household activities and managing children. Women have never been part of the mainstream society in India and they are still considered as a great liability. In other words, women are completely marginalized in India.

Female infanticide is one of the biggest crimes against humanity that is being carried out in India. The patriarchal system encourages a male child and considers women as a property or liability from the day she is born. We need to accept the truth that there is a great discrepancy in the ideology and the actual practice of empowerment policy in India. Everything is happening at a very superficial level and the time has come to find out an actionable path at the ground level for real and measurable change. Women empowerment cannot take place unless women come together and decide to self-empower themselves.

Simone de Beauvoir has given a full-length commentary on the plight of women today. It is worthwhile to quote the author on this subject: "The women of today are in a fair way to dethrone the myth of femininity; they are beginning to affirm their independence in concrete ways; but they do not easily succeed in living completely the life of a human being. Reared by women, which still means practically subordinate to man, for masculine prestige is far from extinction, resting still, on economic and social foundation.

Literature often provides social evidence. We can learn about any society through novels which can give an insight into its culture. Novel is the microcosm of life. The study of society through novels deals with a deep understanding of the status of women in a particular milieu. Novel form is the critical and realistic examination of a society's claims and practices. The novelist has the perception and the analytical mind of a sociologist who provides an exact record of human life, society and the social system. In order to understand the plight of women in the society through fiction, it is essential to find out what issues and problems the novelists raise in their works.

The Hindu moral code known as *The Laws of Manu* denies woman an existence apart from that of husband or his family. Since the publication of Bankim Chandra Chatterjee's *Rajmohan's Wife* in 1864 a significant number of authors have portrayed Indian women as long suffering wives and mothers silenced by patriarchy. The ideal of the traditional, oppressed woman persisted in a culture permeated by religious images of virtuous goddesses devoted to their husbands, the Hindu goddesses Sita, Savitri and Sumati serving as powerful cultural ideals for women. In mythical terms, the dominant feminine prototype is the chaste, patient, self-denying wife, Sita, supported by other figures such as Savitri, Draupadi and Gandhari. When looking at these narratives, silence/speech can be a useful guide to interpreting women's responses to patriarchal hegemony. Silence is a symbol of oppression, a characteristic of the subaltern condition, while speech signifies self-expression and liberation.

The women writers play the role of a social critic, as no writer can isolate herself or himself from society, the violence, the system, the injustice around her. By giving voice to the discontent among middle class women, and creating characters who move from victimization to self-assertion, these writers provide a pattern for the consciousness of the contemporary Indian women. The novels by these women writers cannot destroy repressive social structures; but by raising questions, suggesting reassessment and re-thinking, they can help in formulating a consciousness which can ultimately bring about a constructive and healthy change in society. The novels explored here have in their own way, created such a consciousness. The characters in their novels have often become mouthpieces to voice the writer's own self, thoughts, attitude, ideologies and at other times her experiences, incidents, events and problems that have been seen in her social milieu.

The image of women in fiction has undergone a change during the last four decades. Women writers have moved away from traditional portrayals of enduring, self-sacrificing women searching for identity, no longer characterized and defined simply in terms of their victim status. In contrast to earlier novels, female characters from the 1980s onward assert themselves and defy marriage and motherhood. Contemporary women novelists are closer to the reality, to the subtle nuances of social behaviour, to the complex structures of man and woman's inner life, and to the use of a language that varies from the pedestrian and prosaic to the poetic and ornate.

Recent writers depict both the diversity of women and the diversity within each woman, rather than limiting the lives of women to one ideal. The novels emerging in the 21st century furnish examples of a whole range of attitudes towards the imposition of tradition, some offering an analysis of the family structure and the caste system as the key elements of patriarchal social organization. They also re-interpret mythology by using new symbols and subverting the canonic versions. In conclusion, the work of Indian women writers is significant in making society aware of women's demands, and in providing a medium for self-expression and, thus, re-writing the history of India.

Indian women writers have started questioning the prominent old patriarchal domination. They are no longer puppets in the hands of man. They have shown their worth in the field of literature both qualitatively and quantitatively and are showing it even today without any hurdle. Today, the works of Kamala Markandaya, Nayantara Sahgal, Anita Desai, Geetha Hariharan, Shashi Deshpande, Kiran Desai, Manju Kapur and many more have left an indelible imprint on the readers of Indian fiction in English.

A major development in modern Indian fiction is the growth of a feminist or women-centred approach, that seeks to project and interpret experience, from the point of a feminine consciousness and sensibility. Many Indian women novelists have explored female subjectivity in order to establish an identity. The theme is from childhood to womanhood-developed society respecting women in general.

The image of women in fiction has undergone a change during the last four decades. Women writers have moved away from traditional portrayals of enduring self-sacrificing women, towards conflicts, female characters searching for identity; no longer characterized and defined simply in terms of their victim status. A major preoccupation in recent Indian women's writing has been a delineation of inner life and subtle interpersonal relationships. In a culture where individualism and protest have often remained alien ideas and marital bliss and woman's rolc at home is a central focus. Women's presentation is more assertive, more liberated in their view and more articulate in their expression than the woman of the past is.

The last three decades have seen the emergence of woman characterization in Indian literature. To begin with Shashi Deshpande:

> She has projected objectively a new female face with subjective experiences with a geocentric vision. She reflects on the problems and concerns of the middle class Indian women. Her novel *A Matter of Time* is a continuation of her exploration into the many facts of the feminine experience in writing. In this novel she displayed the themes of silence, gender differences, passive suffering and familiar relationships into much deeper realms. The pain of disintegration of the family troubles Aru, who considers herself for her father's action and sets out to undo it.

In her novels, three types of suffering women characters reoccur with subtle changes. The first type belongs to the protagonist's mother or the mother figure, the traditional woman, who believes that her place is with her husband and family. The second type of woman is bolder, more self-reliant and rebellious. She cannot conform to mythological, submissive and surrender vision of womanhood. As radical feminist, ideology expressed, for example, Sarah's friend Nathan in *The Dark Holds No Terrors*.

The third type of women characters, are the women in-between neither traditional nor radical in their ideas and practice. For example, Indu in *Roots and Shadows* leaves her husband to seek refuge in her ancestral home. Being a woman herself, she sympathizes with women. As Shashi Deshpande clarifies in one of the interviews about feminist approach in her writing, "If others see something feminist in my writings, I must say that it is not consciously done. It is because the world for women is like that and I am mirroring the world."

The other noted novelist is Manju Kapur. Her novel *A Married Woman* is a seductive story of a love at a time of political and religious upheaval, and is told with sympathy and intelligence. *A Married Woman* is the story of an artist whose canvas challenges the constraints of middle-class existence. Manju

Kapur describes through her protagonist Astha: "A woman should be aware of self-controlled, strong-willed, self-reliant and rational, having faith in the inner strength of womanhood. A meaningful change can be brought only from within by being free in the deeper psychic sense."

Astha like to have a break from dependence on others and proceeds on the path of full human status that poses a threat to Hemant and his male superiority. However, she finds herself trapped between the pressures of the modern developing society and shackles of ancient biases. She sets out her quest for a more meaningful life in her lesbian relationship. She canonizes and commemorates her insulted feminine sensibility raising the male tantrum to social transformation in the society.

Manju Kapoor in *Difficult Daughters* presents the image of suffering women. In postcolonial era, partition has ever been the most prolific and prominent area for creative writers. During this phase, a number of novels were written on the theme of destruction. It provides a sad telling commentary on the breakdown of human values. In her writings, Manju Kapoor has emphasized the issues in the context of patriarchy; inter-religious marriage; family bond, male-female bond, co-existence of past and present. She has narrated her women protagonists as a victim of biology, gender, domestic violence, and circumstances. Kapoor thinks: "There is a man within every woman and a woman in every man. When, manhood is questioned womanhood is fragmented."

Anita Nair in her novel *Ladies Coupe*, through the intimate conversation among the women of the ladies coupe portrays a fairly large part of society of all socio-economic levels and age groups. The moral dilemmas of women trapped in social and emotional circumstances, struggling against oppression and a hostile fate are very well interpreted. The novel has the central character Akhila and her live co-passengers which the novelist draws out—these are Janaki, Margaret, Prabha Devi, Sheela and Manikolanthu. Each one is chosen for a specific facet to be projected, each exerting a deep influence on Akhila's decision to marry or stay single at the age of forty-five. The realistic picture of the humble and miserable lives of urban domestic help, their destitution and injustice is presented through Marikilanthu.

In the sad, toilsome and exploited life of man, Anita Nair exposes the practical motives which govern human actions bringing a touch of brutal honesty to the complicated lives of women. Anita Nair has delicately brought up the issues of child abuse when fourteen-year-old Sheela wonders why one of her friend's father behaves like that, touching her and why Ammamma forbids her going there. Anita Nair gives her observations on society. The central character's interaction with the others helps her understand herself better. Through introspection and analysis, she enters a new phase of self-realization and assertion.

Can a woman stay single and be happy? Can a woman do whatever she wants to do without bothering about social approval? These are the questions hinted upon to examine the validity of the rubrics of conservative value system which dictates the way women should lead their lives. Akhila is a clerk in the Income Tax Department and she is the breadwinner of the family. She is the cash cow, but nobody takes care of her or her needs. At the end of the journey, Akhila learns that it is in her hands to create happiness and nobody would come and bring satisfaction in her life. She learns to change the course of her journey according to her wish without bothering about social approval. She understands that those who are ready to pin-point a person when a rule is broken will not come forward in times of need. So, there is no point in following its outdated and meaningless rules. That's why at the end of the novel, Akhila calls up Ian, once her lover, and almost eight years younger to her. Now, she understands that she need not follow social conventions when they don't owe her joy and pleasure. She feels empowered and what really matters to her, is that, now "she throws her head back and voices her triumph."

Kavery Nambisan, in her novel *The Hills of Angheri* is vocal in her critiques of urban-centred health planning. She is critical of the ills plaguing the Indian healthcare system and the problem of female foeticide. In the novel, the protagonist Nalli suffers all taboos prevalent in society to become a doctor, escaping the fate of an early marriage and the burden of preconceived notions. Nalli is reproved for her ambitions. Her elders tell her that if God wanted her to be a doctor, he would have made her a boy. Nambisan admits that such words were said to her when she wanted to become a doctor. She says that in conservative families, girls do not do medicine, they do something easier. But she was determined to be a doctor and wanted to work in rural areas. Nambisan's dreams, fears, joys and sorrows in her life's journey are reflected in Nalli's journey from a little village girl to a confident doctor on the pages of the novel. Nalli fights her family in pursuing her dream of becoming a doctor and setting up her own hospital at Angheri, along with her childhood sweetheart Jai.

Nalli is not deterred even when Jai agrees with everybody that even if she becomes a doctor, she will wear medical degree as an ornament around her neck and ultimately she will be somebody's wife. Such is the fate of village girls in some societies in India, when their dreams are squashed by such cruel words. When her brother Budhi gets jaundice, Angheri's vaidyar comments that their village needs a doctor of the right kind. Nalli's appa, the village school master, starts thinking and Nalli gets an ally in her quest. Throughout the six years of pursuing the medical career, her longing for Angheri's hills continues. On completing her course, Nalli wants to become a surgeon. Appa borrows money to pay for her ticket to England. Through the training in Liverpool, she learns fast, gains confidence and fights racial discrimination when a patient does not want to be treated by an Asian doctor. She learns that as a doctor she not have the luxury of making mistakes. In her profession, there is no place for indecision or doubts. She also learns that to be a successful surgeon, one should not expect someone to hold one's hand.

Likewise many Indian women novelists have explored female subjectivity in order to establish an identity that is not imposed by a patriarchal society. Thus, the theme of growing up from childhood to womanhood, that is, the Bildungsroman, is a recurrent strategy. Santha Rama Rau's *Remember the House*, Ruth Pawar Jhabvala's first novel *To Whom She Will* and her later *Heat and Dust* which was awarded Booker Prize, and Kamala Markandaya's *Two Virgins* are good examples. As in poetry, the image of the New Woman and her struggle for an identity of her own also emerges in the Indian English novel. Such a struggle uses this theme as the nucleus of *Rich like Us*. Other novels, such as Rama Mehta's *Inside the Haveli*, look more towards issues of traditional Indian culture, particularly the debate on female education. Another example of the western educated female protagonist's quest for her cultural roots is Githa Hariharan's *The Thousand Faces of Night*.

Anita Desai, in her psychological novels, presents the image of a suffering woman preoccupied with her sulking frustration and the storm within: the existential predicament of a woman in a male-dominated society. Through such characters, she makes a plea for a better way of life for women.

In her novels, she enacts not only the courageous attempts of individuals to emancipate themselves from inherited cultural and social bonds but also her own freedom as artist; the shifting contours of everyday life throw up new locations of truth, and constitute the fertile ground of fiction itself. In her fictional revelations about the truth of women's lives in India, Desai shows that for her women characters, 'at home' in India all too frequently means the confinement to a domestic milieu, and the bearing of an intolerable cultural tradition. This is the experience of Nanda Kaul in *Fire on the Mountain*, and Bim and Tara in *Clear Light of the Day*. These woman protagonists have connived in their own imprisonment in the sense that Desai has argued, that they have accepted the grind of domesticity in a familial and cultural situation when other choices do not seem available or the opportunity for seeking them out does not arise, and being an outcast is unthinkable.

Sultry Days by Shobha De is the most striking attempt in propagating the idea of female subjectivity, which is not just a slavish succumbing to male dominance but every woman is a staunch feminist in her heart resisting male injustices. In her novel, a victimized woman is presented to face life in a struggling yet confident manner. The novel infers that a woman with a fully integrated personality can solve many problems in her life and she need not be a victim, a fact manifested through the powerfully drawn character of Nisha Verma.

Sultry Days ends on a note of optimism for the women folk belonging to the upper-middle class Indian milieu. Nisha learns to be courageous from her mother and both the women begin to sustain the men in their lives. In the novel, while hollowness of the class difference is shattered consistently, the folly of accepting the slavish subjectivity of women to male dominance is brought out, at the same time the feminine consciousness with its sustaining and pathological impact on family, community and society is proved time and again.

Female subjectivity is one of the most regressive elements in a social set up. The women long for love, dependency and the material and emotional comfort of fixed class identity. At the same time there is the ardent desire to be autonomous, so she is torn between the two and suffers quietly "constraints of bourgeois femininity" and oscillates between "reason and desire, autonomy and dependent security, psychic and social identity."

It is thought that women have become empowered through collective reflection and decision-making, also by building a positive self-image, understanding the conditions and causes of their subordination, developing ability to think critically and ensuring equal participation in the process and bringing about change in society. In studying the problematic of women's empowerment we are faced with questions like: Despite all claims that woman takes charge of her destiny, is she really free? The fact is that questions of women's empowerment arise especially in those societies that are labelled as under-developed. The contemporary women writers can help in the significant task of deconstructing redefining or demolishing the gender archetypes that the society has created through centuries.

Works Cited

Joshi, Padmakar. *Shashi Deshpande's Fiction: A Study in Women Empowerment and Postcolonial Discourse*. New Delhi: Prestige.

Kapoor, Manju. *Difficult Daughters*. Noida: Gopsons, 1998.

http://shodhganga.inflibnet.ac.in:8080/jspui/bitstream/10603/8047/7/07_chapter%201.pdf

http://www.ukessays.com/essays/english-literature/women-empowerment-in-indian-english-novels-english-literature-essay.php

En.wikipedia.org/wiki/Women_in_India

Nair, Anita. *Ladies Coupe*. New Delhi: Penguin, 2001.

Nambisan, Kavery. *The Hills of Angheri*. New Delhi: Penguin, 2005.

Desai, Anita. *Fire on the Mountain*, London: Penguin, 1977.

Deshpande, Shashi. *The Dark Holds No Terrors*, New Delhi: Penguin, 1990.

De, Shobha. *Sultry Days*. New Delhi: Penguin, 1994.

Why Feminism?
Why not Humanism or Equalism?

PRIVIETHA
Dr. Sivanthi Aditanar College of Education, Tiruchendur

Feminism is the radical notion that women are people.
Cheris Kramarae and Paula Treichler

Feminism is a recognition and critique of male supremacy combined with efforts to change it. Feminists fight for the equality of women and argue that women should share equally in society's opportunities and scarce resources. According to Tess Lantos, "Feminism is a movement that includes women and men who wish to see a world where discrimination based on gender and the idea that men are superior to women is abolished."

The first wave of feminism took place in the late nineteenth and early twentieth centuries, emerging out of an environment of urban industrialism and liberal, socialist politics. The goal of this wave was to open up opportunities for women, with a focus on suffrage. Discussions about the vote and women's participation in politics led to an examination of the differences between men and women as they were then viewed. Some claimed that women were morally superior to men and so their presence in the civic sphere would improve public behaviour and the political process. The major goals of the first wave of feminism are suffrage/ right to vote, public participation in democracy and economic opportunity

The second wave began in the 1960s and continued into the 1990s. This wave unfolded in the context of the anti-war and civil rights movements and the growing self-consciousness of a variety of minority groups around the world. The New Left was on the rise and the voice of the second wave was increasingly radical. In this phase, sexuality and reproductive rights were dominant issues and much of the movement's energy was focused on passing the Equal Rights Amendment to the Constitution guaranteeing social equality regardless of sex. The major goals of the second wave of feminism are sexual and reproductive rights, job and harassment protection for women, challenges of the domestic/ traditional role for women, access to education and Equal Rights Amendment

The third wave of feminism began in the mid of 1990s and was informed by postcolonial and postmodern thinking. In this phase many constructs were destabilized, including the notions of "universal womanhood," body, gender and sexuality. Most third-wavers refuse to identify as "feminists" and reject the word that they find limiting and exclusionary. Girl-feminism tends to be global, multicultural, and it shuns simple answers or artificial categories of identity, gender, and sexuality. Its transversal politics means that differences such as those of ethnicity, class, sexual orientation, etc. are celebrated and recognized as dynamic, situational, and provisional. Third wave feminism breaks boundaries. The major goals of the third wave of feminism was to welcome with open arms the feminine form, recognition of different racial experiences among women, the trans-gender/trans-sexuality and the many kinds of sexuality and self-acceptance.

There are many kinds of feminism. The common models of feminism are Liberal Feminism, Radical Feminism, Marxist and Socialist Feminism, Cultural Feminism and Eco-Feminism.

Liberal Feminism sprung out of the civil rights and peace movements in 1967-1968. It aims to achieve equal legal, political and social rights for women. It wishes to bring women equality into all public institution and to extend the creation of knowledge so that women's issues can no longer be ignored. Feminists strive for sexual equality via down-to-earth political and legal reform. Liberal feminism is a form of feminism that argues that equality for women can be achieved through legal means and social reform.

Radical feminism is a movement that believes sexism is so deeply rooted in society that the only cure is to eliminate the concept of gender completely. Radical feminists argue that the entire traditional family system is sexist. Men are expected to work outside the home while women are expected to take care of children and clean the house.

The reason this group gets the "radical" label is that it views oppression of women as the most fundamental form of oppression, one that cuts across boundaries of race, culture and economic class. This is a movement intent on social change, change of rather revolutionary proportions, in fact.

Marxism recognizes that women are oppressed and attributes the oppression to the capitalist/ private property system. Thus it insists that the only way to end oppression of women is to overthrow the capitalist system.

Socialist feminism is the result of Marxism meeting radical feminism. Socialist feminists reject radical feminism's main claim that patriarchy is the only or primary source of oppression of women. Rather, socialist feminists assert that women are unable to be free due to their financial dependence on males in society.

Women are subject to the male rulers in capitalism due to an uneven balance in wealth. They argue that liberation can only be achieved by working to end both the economic and cultural sources of women's oppression.

As radical feminism died out as a movement, cultural feminism got rolling. In fact, many of the same people moved from the former to the latter. They carried the name "radical feminism" with them, and some cultural feminists use that name still.

Cultural feminism believes in encouraging feminine behaviour rather than masculine behaviour. For example, the belief that "women are kinder and gentler than men," prompts cultural feminists' call for an invasion of women's culture into the male-dominated world, which would presumably result in less violence and fewer wars.

Eco-feminism is a social and political movement which unites environmentalism and feminism. This branch of feminism is much more spiritual than political or theoretical in nature. It may or may not be wrapped up with Goddess worship and vegetarianism. Parallels are often drawn between society's treatment of the environment, animals, or resources and its treatment of women. In resisting patriarchal culture, eco-feminists feel that they are also resisting plundering and destroying the Earth. Eco-feminists believe that these connections are illustrated through traditionally "female" values such as reciprocity, nurturing and cooperation, which are present both among women and in nature. We need feminism because

- Women deserve equal pay for equal work
- For considering women as object
- Gender inequality is literally bad for women's health
- Equal status for men and women
- Child marriages are still common
- Women are still defined mostly by looks.
- Women are mostly the stay-at-home parent.
- Forced prostitution is a booming business.
- Sexual harassment in employment exists, everywhere.

Feminism is not just about women, it's about men too. Both men and women are judged on certain parameters as stated. We need Feminism because there are still some restrictions for women: do not wear certain types of clothes, do not travel alone, give up your career for marriage, learn household jobs perfectly, adjust and continue if you are not happy in your marriage.

Feminism is a struggle for equality of women, an effort to make women become like men. The agonistic definition of feminism sees it as the struggle against all forms of patriarchal and sexiest aggression. The main goal of feminism is to oppose woman to be treated as a sex object and to provide equality with man. She must be treated as a human being and not an object for male-gratification. Feminism is to change the mindset that the world is a place to live for both men and women.

Bibliography

Das, Krishan and Deepchand Patra. (2009). *Studies in Women Writers in English*. New Delhi: Commonwealth Publishers.

Moi, Toril. (1989). "Feminist, Female, Feminine." *The Feminist Reader: Essays in Gender and the Politics of Literary Criticism*, ed. Catherine Belsey and Jane Moore. New York: Basil Blackwell.

Scholz, Sally J. (2011). *Feminism: A Beginner's Guide*. New York: Oneworld.

Tandon, Neeru. (2008). *Feminism: A Paradigm Shift*. New Delhi: Atlantic.

http://www.landfield.com/faqs/feminism.html

http://www.ifeminists.net/introduction.html

http://www.uah.edu/woolf/feminism_kinds.html

http://www.amptoons.com/blog/2005/02/23/what-distinguishes-each-form-of-feminism-from-thehttp://www.redletterpress.org/feminism 101. html

The Position of Woman: Recognition, Representation and Reformation in Fourth World Literature

SARALA DEVI MANUKONDA
SDM Siddartha Mahila Kalasala, Vijayawada

> As a woman, I have no country. As a woman, I want no country. As a woman, my country is my world. (Virginia Woolf)

It predates the coinage of the word 'Fourth World' and its epistemological origins and in fact should have been its primary constituency after inception, but was acknowledged only much later, as by its sheer definition; the constituency of 'Women' and their centuries of struggle, falls within its ambit. The fact that it was felt essential by women of the times to bring out a 'Declaration of Rights of Women and the Female Citizen' (1791),' as soon as 'The Declaration of the Rights of Man and of the Citizen (1789)'—a fundamental document in the history of Human Rights—was released, proves that women felt that their basic rights as 'woman' were addressed neither in the rights of 'man' nor in the rights of 'citizens.' The women fought and sacrificed along with the men for the liberation of man; only to realize that the declaration—"all men are born free and equal in rights"—does not include woman. The contributions of women in all the struggles and movements for liberation/ emancipation of 'man,' are invisibilized, so are their rights to equality.

The culture of patriarchy in all its various hues across the world is the primary force that drives this refusal to acknowledge the rights of women. Patriarchy was intentionally embedded into societal structures through language, religion and traditions and over thousands of years, made it invisible. It is the cultural constructs of patriarchy that perpetuate the image of woman as irrational, emotional, hysterical, and a body without boundaries and hence needs to be under the control of man through all stages of her life. This control is exercised in such an inhuman manner, that the differentiation, discrimination, subjugation, exploitation and even elimination starts from the time a female foetus is conceived and continues till her death and this differentiation leads to innumerable crimes against the girl child and women. Since awakenings of the fraternity of women across the globe, conceptualized in the 'Declaration of Rights of Women and the Female Citizen' and innumerable, heart-wrenching struggles for centuries; achieved equal rights and status for themselves, constitutionally and legally—at least in most nations. But the culture of patriarchy supersedes even the laws and statutes and the attainment of justice is undermined at all levels, even by women themselves as they are already complicit in their own subjugation, through patriarchal cultural constructs such as 'Pativrata' and ideologies such as 'Streedharma,' in the Indian context. Simone de Beauvoir (1949) puts it succinctly when she states: 'Qualities associated with the concept of woman were fabricated, culturally constructed, an artifact of patriarchy, by a society that benefitted from keeping women subordinate and not because of any natural or essential qualities inherent in being a woman.'

'The Subaltern cannot speak,' says Gayatri Chakravorty Spivak (1988). The formally accepted primary constituents of the Fourth World are the indigenous, aboriginal, tribal and all other marginalized communities of the world. In the Indian context it is primarily the dalits and adivasis, whose ignoble lives are well documented and whose struggles since Indian independence, led to the framing of laws and statutes and their implementation however partially. The participation of dalit and adivasi women in the struggles for securing the rights of their communities is well documented too, but the status of women within these communities remains the most abysmal. The overbearing force of patriarchy intersects with the forces of casteism and feudalism to create the lowest category of the Fourth World, which is marked by the social, physical, economic and political exploitation of dalit women. They are thrice oppressed by caste, gender and class and this creates multi-dimensionality and simultaneity of oppression, thus increases its intensity. Aruna Gnanadason tersely states, 'Dalit women are the dalit in Indian society—Dalit women in India live a precarious existence combining abject poverty with grinding labour in the fields and workplaces; and in the home they are abused and used, powerless and exploited.' Dalit women, who constitute 16% of the female population of India, remain the most economically unprivileged, socially outcaste, culturally subservient, politically powerless and always perceived as the 'other.'

The post-independence women's movements in India focused on women's equal rights, equal pay, violence against women in and out of the home and other issues. Indian women were assumed as a homogeneous category as it was organized and mentored by middle class, upper caste women. The specificity of dalit women's oppression remained hidden and thus the subjects of marginalization of women in the development process, contribution of women in the unorganized sector and feminization of poverty are discussed without even referring to the specificity that they are all about dalit women. This continued till the dalit women were forced to form autonomous groups which started working as cooperative community groups to help themselves, stand their ground against all kinds of oppression and be heard individually and collectively.

The cultural constructs of patriarchy modulate almost every aspect of our society, viz. religion, economy, state, family and individual identity. They limit the feminine existence to such an extent that it becomes invisible and it takes an effort to even explore feminine ways of being. Culture even blinds the Fourth World to the plight of their own women, it limits the acceptability of creating gender equality and thus the men of the Fourth World have no compunctions in using religious and caste traditions to perpetuate gender discrimination. The patriarchal caste hierarchy controls women's sexuality, for maintaining caste purity and controlling inheritance and hence women are considered the gateways to caste and the regulatory authority for perpetuating this culture. This makes it almost impossible for women to articulate their own visions of emancipation, much less work towards achieving them.

'Dalit women speak differently,' says Gopal Guru. Language is the primary building block of culture and culture is primarily represented in literature. A brief review of Fourth World literature reveals that it is the result of revolt and a long struggle of the oppressed and marginalized people. Dalit literature is associated with a movement to bring about change. However, Dalit male literature fell prey to two ideological structures—one which sees women as natural, spontaneous and primordial, while the other makes them an indivisible part of oppressed human society. The former exalts them as idol, while the later marks them off as invisible. The voices of the women within this literature are nowhere to be heard; for they haven't found their voice yet. The voices of this deprived constituent of the Fourth World came to be heard first as voices of the anguished in the form of autobiographies, epitomized by Maya Angelou who has written a series of six autobiographical volumes on her experience as a black woman in America and in India by Bama's autobiography, *Karukku,* which details her life struggles as a Dalit woman. Thcsc autobiographies are sociologically enlightening, politically subverting and aesthetically interesting, for the simple reason that dalit women writing is utterly realistic. The differentiating factor is the language used which is direct, forthright, candid, expletive and brutally honest. The highlight is the difference of the women of their communities from women of the mainstream society, the irrelevance of feminist ideology to their own experiences, and the finality that it is upto themselves to take their lives into their own hands and work together for their own emancipation. Their voice is not singular but contains a multiplicity of voices that intersect at similar experiences. The deluge of Fourth world women's literature that followed expanded into narration of the lives of other dalit women, in other words biographies as fiction. But as Arundhati Roy states: 'Fiction is truth. In fact the absolute truth.' The fiction of Alice Walker, Joyce Carol Oates, Toni Morrison, Elfriede Jelinek, Alice Munro, Bama, Mahasweta Devi, Urmila Pawar, Sharmila Rege, Sumitr Bhave, Baby Kamble and Shantabai Kamble are not so different; if the Indian dalit women write about issues of caste and gender subjugation, the western women write about issues of racist and sexist oppression. With their identity established and their voices made audible; the dalit women's struggle intensified, using the leverage they have as hard-working earning members of their families and certain cultural liberties within their communities they overcame even the rural-urban divide.

The autonomous women's movements influenced by secular values were unwilling to take on religion and patriarchy proactively. However the movements did get reflected in literature as most of the activists are authors and they converted live data into meaningful theory. Gabriele Dietrich, Gail Omvedt and Ilina Sen are all activists involved with various women's movements in different parts of India. Their research and analysis concludes that women's movements need to go beyond women's issues to include issues of development, ecology and religion. Omvedt documented how rural women are at the forefront of new alternatives, as they are reworking issues of gender, caste, ecology and rural livelihoods through their focus on 'stree shakti' or women's power, rather than on women's oppression. Their alternate model of development is based on biomass production, renewable energy sources, skilled employment in rural areas and seeking property rights as well as political power at the local level. Dietrich's writings on autonomous women's movements highlight two issues: 'One is how to draw on women's vital experiences and skills to reverse the situation of oppression and the other is to work out the connection between the ecological and the cultural crises caused by development based on a neo-colonial, capitalist, patriarchal model that violently assaults the base for human material and spiritual survival, and is destructive of both nature and culture.' The lives of dalit women are intrinsically linked to natural resources which are seriously affected by political and economical decisions of the nation.

'Earth itself has become the nigger of the world,' says Alice Walker (1983). Karen Warren lists eight forms of woman-nature connections, elaborated as historical, conceptual, empirical, symbolic, epistemological, political, ethical and theoretical connections.

1. Historical connections date back to 4500 B.C. to the invasion of Indo-European societies by nomadic tribes from Eurasia, which shifted the matrifocal, matrilineal, peaceful agrarian societies to patriarchal ones. Classical Greek philosophical concepts of rationality are another connection. But it was during the sixteenth and seventeenth centuries' industrial revolution that the reductionist, mechanistic worldview took hold, which paved the way for the exploitation of nature and the subordination of women.
2. Conceptual connections can be noticed in the value dualisms in disjunctive pairs which are seen as opposite and exclusive. Emotion, body and nature are associated with woman and are inferior to reason, mind and culture associated with man. These value dualisms then got extrapolated on other oppressive frameworks of sexism, racism, classism and naturism, i.e., the domination of non-human nature. The sex-gender

differences and the development of differentiated personality and consciousness is another conceptual connection.

3. Empirical connections are deduced from the economic policies of the First World that impact food, forest and water and contribute to the inability of women to provide themselves and their families. The health risks due to low-level radiation, pesticides and toxic pollutants are disproportionately borne by poor women and children. Animal farming and experimentation, hunting and meat eating are concepts and practices which are patriarchal derivatives, so also are sexual assault and pornography.
4. Symbolic connections between women-nature are seen in language, literature, art, religion and theology. Language inferiorizes women and non-human nature by naturalizing women and feminizing nature. Women are described using terms like cows, foxes, chicks, snakes, bitches, beavers, old bats, cats, bird-brained, hare-brained. Nature is described in sexist terms like conquered, controlled, mined, mastered, raped and phrases like 'her secrets are penetrated,' 'her womb is put into the service of the man of science,' 'virgin forest/ timber,' 'fertile soil,' 'barren land.' Language describes, reflects and perpetuates the domination and inferiorization of both women and nature, which are analogous not only figuratively, but also culturally. These patriarchal conceptions justify the domination and exploitation of earth and women.
5. Epistemological connections explore the notions of human self as separate from nature, instrumental view of nature, environmental ethics and politics of instrumentalism. Critical connections point to the convergence of feminist and ecological concerns, nature versus culture dichotomy and a theoretical structure for analyzing the relationships between the domination of women and the domination of culture.

6. Political connections examine the grassroots political movements of anti-dam, anti-nuclear, anti-militarist, peace, ecology, environmental health, animal rights, species parity, etc. and the potential of women movements for analyzing the domination, explaining, clarifying and guiding the ecological revolution and implementing pro-nature policies.
7. Ethical connections scrutinize the interconnectedness of women and nature and environmental ethics, for evolving a feminist ethical analysis and response; as mainstream environmental ethics are anthropocentric and androcentric.
8. Theoretical connections can be noticed in the competing theories in all areas of feminist and environmental thought as evidenced in the field of environmental ethics.

Women bear the brunt of economic and social consequences of climate change as destruction of the environment results in the elimination of women's method to survival. No wonder then that women have been at the forefront of ecological movements starting from Chipko Movement (1974-India) and Green Belt Movement (1977-Kenya) to Navadanya Movement (Ongoing-India). Women also suffer disproportionately during extreme climatic catastrophes like cyclones, floods, drught, and earthquakes, due to cultural deprivation of coping strategies and are subjected to intimidation and gender-based violence during and after rescue and relief operations; innumerable instances of which are documented worldwide, especially in the Third World.

> Women must see that there can be no liberation for them and no solution to the ecological crisis within a society whose fundamental model of relationships continues to be one of domination. They must unite the demands of the women's movement with those of the ecological movement to envision a radical reshaping of the basic socio-economic relations and the underlying values of this [modern industrial] society. (Warren)

Women play a much stronger role than men in the management of ecosystem services and food security.' (Achim Steiner, Under-Secretary General, UNEP [2011]) The connections between women and ecology reveal that they are natural allies which synergize each other. Ecofeminism is a feminist approach to ecology, which exposes and tries to dismantle the structures of hierarchy and domination, commodification of nature and women, and colonization of nature and marginalized humans; concepts which echo in the Fourth World. It is a realization that we have exceeded the environmental limits our earth can bear and recognition that the subjugation and exploitation of women is intrinsically linked to notions of class, caste, race, neo-colonialism, neo-capitalism, development and globalization.

> The holism implied in the feminine principle must be distinguished from the universalism of the modern scientific era. The former respects and nurtures diversity; the latter undermines it under its homogenizing and centralizing thrust and, in the end, destroys diversity. There is violence inherent in the development and growth models and are absolutely unsustainable. (Shiva)

Ecofeminism as a theory and movement is articulated by women's movements' activists, who are also scholars and writers; some of whom may be from the economic and social elites, like Karen Warren and Vandana Shiva, but definitely the participants of these emancipatory movements are all constituents of the Fourth World. They challenge the hegemony of androcentricism and anthropocentricism in the name of development, growth and progress; while they devastate earth and enslave entire communities and cultures. They evolve structures that respect difference without universalizing and fully agree with a Fourth World concept that 'the personal is political.' Ecofeminist movements advocate community-based economies, local and sustainable agricultural systems, locally led eco-tourism ventures, fair trade products, local governance and decision-making, and human rights. They oppose animal-based agri-business, provincialism and institutional and state oppression; and work within social movements for 'globalization from below.'.

A review of the recommendations of United Nations Environmental Programme (UNEP) 2011, for governments of all countries and NGOs on the field will help in highlighting why Ecofeminism concepts need to be embraced by the Fourth World. The relevant recommendations of UNEP are as follows:

1. The adaptation programmes for food security, agriculture, rangelands and managing natural resources should have a strong focus on women and gender equity to ensure success. Strengthen adaptation by ensuring women's access, control and ownership of resources (land, livestock, property and income opportunities) and access to development resources such as credit, information, training and out-reach and culturally appropriate and labour-saving technology.
2. Invest in gender sensitive and culturally appropriate labour-saving green technologies, water harvesting, storage and irrigation systems in collaboration with women, to reflect their needs and concerns, while ensuring that physical, cultural, social, economic and practical elements are compatible with their livelihood practices within diverse ecosystems, households and communities.
3. Conduct a systematic analysis of climate change from environment, development and gender equity perspectives to fill urgent gaps in research, knowledge and data—with a distinct focus on women's needs, priorities, constraints, impacts, local strategies, knowledge and meaningful participation.
4. Ensure that education, training, awareness raising and information programmes address the vulnerability and risk of gender-based violence, sexual abuse and trafficking—especially in high-risk flood, drought and disaster prone areas.

A dynamic synchronization and balance of relations between man-woman, human-nature and in fact between our earth and all earthlings, so very essential for sustainability of our civilization, can only be achieved through Ecofeminism. 'As this ecocentric repossession of pastoral has gathered force, its centre of energy has begun to shift from representation of nature as a theatre for human events to representation in the sense of advocacy of nature as a presence for its own sake.' (Buell 1995: 52)

Ecofeminism requires a reconceiving of many normally accepted notions of reason, rationality, knowledge, objectivity, ethics and values from epistemological and ontological perspectives. It also requires further development of gender sensitive language, theory and practice that does not discriminate and perpetuate exploitation of women and nature. Writers, especially women writers need to be sensitive to issues concerning nature and ecology and tread the pastoral tradition in its postmodern form. The contemporary post-pastoral language is ecofeminist in its approach, with a concern for environment, rather than 'countryside' or landscape; a recognition of creative-destructive balance in a continuous momentum of birth and death, death and rebirth, growth and decay, ecstasy and dissolution; a realization that our inner human nature can be understood in relation to external nature; an awareness of both nature as culture and of culture as nature and finally the consciousness that the exploitation of the planet is of the same mindset as the exploitation of women and minorities.

It can be noticed that all the Fourth World female writers have continued to show women as victims, even though they may be resisting victimization. The autobiographies are biographies of pain and can be deeply depressing, with no redemption in sight. Most fiction is semi-autobiographical and hence reflects the writer's cultural moorings, which are still anchored in patriarchal cultural traditions.

Our consciousness gives rise to our conscience, and our conscience should take the responsibility for our behaviour towards other species of the earth and towards the earth itself. The concern for the exploitation of women in terms of gender, religion, caste and class should accompany concern for the environment in terms of species, elements and atmosphere and vice versa. The attainment of a vibrant harmony between man-woman and human-nature and in fact for our earth and all earthlings can only be through ecofeminism. As midwives of understanding the Fourth World writers, nay all writers, should deliver literature in all their forms, poetry, fiction, biographies, autobiographies, scripts for films and TV shows, storyboards for cartoons and of course the blogs; which is ecofeminist in culture. . Ecofeminism in Fourth world literature will have to drive the cultural change led by the postmodern woman (be she dalit or elite and urban or rural), who will depict women as agents and not captives of culture, develop a mature environmental aesthetic with a vision of an integrated natural world that includes the human; towards an emancipated, egalitarian society.

Bibliography

Aranha, Celine, Peter Fernando and Prabha Mahale, *Dalit Women,* New Delhi: Indian Social Institute, 1991.

Bama. *Karukku*, trans. Lakshmi Holmstrom, Chennai, Macmillan, 2000.

_____. *Sangati,* trans. Lakshmi Holmstrom, Chennai, Oxford University Press, 2005.

Chakravarti, Uma, *Conceptualizing Brahminical Patriarchy in Early India*, New Delhi: Centre for Contemporary Studies, Nehru Memorial Museum and Library, 1993.

Datar, Chhaya, *Ecofeminism Revisited,* Jaipur, Rawat, 2011,

Deshpandc, Shashi, *If I Die Today,* New Delhi, Vikas, 1982,

Desai and Krishnaraj Maithreyi, *An Overview of the Status of Women in India,* Meerut: Ajanta, 1987.

Dietrich Gabriele. "Dalit Movements and Women's Movements," *Encyclopedia of Dalits in India*: *Women*, Sanjay Paswan and Pramanshi Jaideva. New Delhi, Kalpaz, 2002.

Gaard, Greta, "New Directions for Ecofeminism: Towards a More Feminist Ecocriticism," *Oxford Journal*, ISLE, 2011.

Guru, Gopal. "Dalit Women Talk Differently," *Economic and Political Weekly*, 2548-50

Gnanadason, Aruna, *Dalit Women—The Dalit of the Dalit*, ed. Nirmal Arvind. Chennai: Lutheran Theological College and Research Institute, 1990.

Miles and Shiva Vandana, *Ecofeminism*, Nova Scotia, Canada: Fernwood, 1993,

Mishra, Jugal Kishore. A Critical Study of Dalit Literature in India, SASNET. http://www.sasnet.lu.se/EASASpapers/4JugalKishore

Patnaik, Bharati, *Identity and Gender,* New Delhi, Commonwealth Publishers, 2013.

Rao, Srinivas and Srinivasulu Reddy, "Fourth World Literature: An Introduction," *Online International Interdisciplinary Research Journal*, Vol. III, Nov. 2013.

Shiva, Vandana, *Staying Alive,* New Delhi, Kali for Women, 1988.

_____, *The Violence of Green Revolution: Ecological Degradation and Political Conflict in Punjab,* New Delhi: Zed Press, 1992.

Singh, Ranjana. "Dalit Women Identity in Bama's *Sangati,*" *The Criterion: An International Journal in English*, October 2013, Vol. 4, Issue V. http://www.thecriterion.com/V4/n5Ranjanapdf

Spivak, Gayatri Chakravorty. "Draupadi by Mahasweta Devi," *Critical Inquiry*, Vol. 8, No. 2, 1981. http://links.jstor.org

Talukdar, Shashwati. *A study guide for the film 'Mahasweta Devi: Witness, Advocate, Writer.'* http://www.der.org/films/mahasweta-devi.html

Tomar, Ruchi. "Dalit Feminism: A Transformation of Rejection into Resistance," *The Criterion: An International Journal in English,* February 2013, Issue 12. http://www.thecriterion.com

Usha, A. "Feminism in Mahasweta Devi's Selected Stories," *National Journal on Advances in Computing and Management*, Vol. 1, No. 1, March 2010. http://www.journals-satyabhama.com

Warren, Karen, *Introduction to Ecofeminism*, ed. Zimmerman, Callicott, Sessions, Warren, and Clark John, *Environmental Philosophy: From Animal Rights to Radical Ecology,* New Jersey: Prentice-Hall, 1993.

The Translation of Terror and Terrorism in Kiran Desai's *The Inheritance of Loss*

HALIMAH MOHAMED ALI
Universiti Sains Malaysia

This essay will discuss the concept of terror and terrorism as portrayed in Kiran Desai's novel *The Inheritance of Loss* (2006) and how it is translated into the everyday lives of the characters in the novel. It will introduce the novel, define terror and terrorism, explain who the Gorkhas are and discuss the novel per say. *The Inheritance of Loss* (2006) is Kiran Desai's second novel and it won the Man Booker Prize for her in 2006. She became the youngest woman to win the Man Booker Prize. The novel also won the 2006 National Book Critics Circle Fiction Award. Desai is the prominent Indian-English novelist Anita Desai's daughter. Brought up and educated in India, England and the US, she resides in the States. Her acclaimed first novel *Hullabaloo in the Guava Orchard (*1998) won the Betty Trask Award.

Desai uses the art of the novel well in order to portray a very serious and contemporary issue. According to Halimah Mohamed Ali, in her book titled *Orientalism from within: Arundhati Roy and Her Contemporaries*:

> The novel is a recently acquired tool of expression in Asia because Asian literature is based upon oral literary tradition. In India, significant contribution to the novel in English started in the 1930s by writers like R.K. Narayan, Mulk Raj Anand, Raja Rao and others. Indian writing in English has evolved since then. From being an unknown corpus it has gained global recognition and attention.

> Salman Rushdie, who won the prestigious Booker Prize in 1982 for his novel *Midnight's Children*, propelled Indian-English literature's international fame. His success placed a new generation of Anglophone Indian writing in English on the world map and ever since then it has prospered. The achievement of the Indian-English novel indicates that the art that was introduced by the West has flourished in Asia. (1)

These new Anglophone Indian-English writers like Desai are hailed as 'Rushdie's Children' as pointed out by Halimah Mohamed Ali (2006) vis-à-vis her unpublished thesis titled "Orientalism from within: A Critical Study of Pandering and Catering to the West in Three Contemporary Indian-English Novels" (33).

Desai uses this 'gift' that has been procured by the Indian-English writers via their master storyteller Rushdie, brilliantly. She discusses an issue that is considered to be taboo to the East while it instigates fear and revulsion of and for the East in the West. This delicate contemporary topic, which is actually like old wine that has been put into new bottles, has been tackled in a very subtle manner by Desai through her portrayal of the Indian past that is connected to violence and violent acts of the Gorkhas in order to demand for a free state in India, in her bid to avoid hurting the sentiments of the Muslim world and the Arabs who are normally connected to terrorist acts around the world. The fact that the Arabs are hailed as terrorists can be proven through the deaths of three prominent Arab leaders, of whom, two were head of states and another one the leader of a terrorist link at the hands of the United States of America which elected to go out on a mission that it labelled as 'War on Terror' in 2001 after the September 11 (9/11), tragedy which shocked both the West and the Other including the Muslims. Two of the Arab leaders Saddam Hussein from Iraq and Osama bin Laden of the Al-Qaeda died at the hands of America, while Muammar Gaddafi of Libya was hunted down and assassinated by his own people. However, the sentiments of hatred for them were instigated and entrenched into the minds of the people by the West. It is probable that the 9/11 tragedy shocked the world so much especially the West, that it led to other incidents which can be viewed as tragedies themselves.

The novel under discussion is a story about an orphan girl named Sai. She falls in love with her tuition teacher who is a member of the Gorkhaland independent fighters. This fact is not known to Sai and her grandfather, a retired judge. The fighters resort to terrorism in order to demand their freedom. While the police resort to terror in subduing the rise of terrorism in Kalimpung per say and Darjeeling as a whole. The romance of Sai and Gyan is not the major theme. Though terrorism lurks at the back of the novel it controls the plot, and Sai's relationship with Gyan. Pankaj Mishra describes the novel well in his review of the book titled *Wounded by the West*,

> Although it focuses on the fate of few powerless individuals, Kiran Desai's extraordinary new novel manages to explore, with intimacy and insight, just about every contemporary international issue: globalization, multiculturalism, economic equality, fundamentalism and terrorist violence. Despite being set in the 1980s, it seems the best kind of post-9/11 novel.

Thus, it is appropriate to discuss Desai's novel in the light of terror and terrorism. The next section will concentrate on defining and explaining terror and terrorism.

I

This section will discuss terror and terrorism. Terror has been defined as,

1**:** a state of intense fear
2*a*: one that inspires fear: SCOURGE
b: a frightening aspect <the *terrors* of invasion>
c: a cause of anxiety: WORRY
d: an appalling person or thing; *especially*: BRAT
3**:** Reign of Terror

> 4: violent or destructive acts (as bombing) committed by groups in order to intimidate a population or government into granting their demands <insurrection and revolutionary *terror*> (Merriam-Webster)

The definition of terror that can be seen above aligns it to fear and violence. Many discourses, be they academic or otherwise, relate terror to terrorism. Thus in order to understand terror we have to understand terrorism because they are intertwined.

According to Muhammad Kamal, "For some time now, many scholars have been engaged with understanding and defining terrorism. This engagement is reflected in the considerable amount of literature produced by them on this topic. Although this body of literature discloses important aspects of terrorism, none of it discusses directly the 'essence' of terrorism. The definitions provided are based on the writers' political discourse rather than their philosophical apprehension of terrorism. They think of terrorism as an act of threatening to destroy an intended target for a political end" (1). He goes on to describe and present the ideas of those scholars and also the Marxist definition of terrorism and in the end of his definition of terrorism he states that the term was first used to "describe the radical and violent political attitude of the Jacobins during the French revolution and its aftermath" (2). Kamal argues that terrorism is not a post-modern political fact. However, since 9/11 the world has tried to understand and know what terrorism means. The stress has been on the cultural production of the act. The cultural production becomes the pivotal point of discourse on terrorism by some individuals (3).

Sudha Setty states that the United Nations has tried to define terrorism since the 1960s. However not all nations in the world agree with the definition provided by the United Nations. This is due to the fact that there are freedom struggles, acts against colonialism carried out by natives that have been subjugated. These acts cannot be labeled as terrorist acts because they are feats that are carried out in the name of freedom and equality.

Alan B. Krueger states that although many people blame terrorism on lack of education and poverty there is not enough concrete proof to determine this (2). Krueger argues: "Most terrorists are not motivated by their own material gain. How could one account for an excess of volunteers or suicide missions if that were the case? Instead terrorists are motivated by political goals that they believe are furthered by their actions. The West is often a target—not because it is rich, but because it is influential and because terrorism has a greater chance of succeeding when it is perpetrated against a democracy than autocracy" (4).

Krueger states that the economy is disrupted because terrorists seek to spread fear (8). Although Krueger argues that terrorism is difficult to define, he states that it is a premeditated, politically motivated violence. The goal of terrorism is to spread fear (14-15). There is a relevancy to the communities from which terrorists arise as well as their views. It does not occur in a vacuum (23). Terrorists are motivated by a goal. They are willing to die for the cause that they believe in (48). Krueger informs us that, "88 percent of the time, terrorist attacks occur in the perpetrators' own country of origin" (71).

Ashis Nandy defines terrorism: "Existing theoretical and empirical work stresses two differentiate of contemporary terrorism. First, terrorism is primarily a psychological weapon: 'its purpose to instill fear in an attempt to reach specific objectives.' Second, terrorism is 'essentially indiscriminate' and its choice of victims as arbitrary or random. The lack of discrimination helps to spread fear, for if no one in particular is the target, no one can be safe" (24). He comments on the subject of terrorism in South Asia. He argues that modern terrorism and counter terrorism have become consumer fodder for the middle class. It is possible to sell it, advertise it and purchase it as a "political spectacle and as a commodity through the TV, the newspapers, the radio and commercial films" (23). He argues that it cannot survive without publicity and flourishes due to media exposure (23).

From the discussions above we can conclude that terror and terrorism are synonymous. Terror is a state that occurs after terrorism takes place most of the time. This idea of terror and terrorism can be detected in Desai's the *Inheritance of Loss*. The acts of terrorism instill fear (terror) in the minds and selves of the people living in Kalimpung.

The novel discussed portrays the Gorkhas and their mission to attain a nation state for themselves. It is important for us to know who these people are. According to Munish Tamang and Bharatiya Prasingh,

> Indian Gorkhas are indigenous people living all along the Himalayan belt and the North-East states of India. The Gorkhas inhabit areas in J&K, Himachal, Uttarakhand, Sikkim, Darjeeling, Assam, and all other states in the North-East region of India. In all of these regions the Gorkhas have a long history going back to the pre-independence days.

The Gorkhas have demanded for Gorkhaland based on the provision in Article 3 (a) of the Constitution of India. Article 3 (a) states:

> 3. Formation of new States and alteration of areas, boundaries or names of existing States.—Parliament may by law—
> (a) form a new State by separation of territory from any State or by uniting two or more States or parts of States or by uniting any territory to a part of any State. (*Ibid.*)

Tamang and Prasingh argue that the Gorkhas have never wanted a separate state from India. The demand for Gorkhaland means a state for themselves which is within India. They want it created from Bengal like Gujarat was created from Bombay, Haryana from Punjab and Andhra Pradesh out of Madras to name a few. Tamang and Prasingh state that like the other states which have enriched India so will Gorkhaland. (*Ibid.*)

There was an agitation in Darjeeling in 1986 instigated by the Gorkhas through the Gorkha National Liberation Front (GNLF) demanding for their own nation state as depicted in Desai's *The Inheritance of Loss*. About 1,200 people were killed throughout the period of the agitation. Due to the agitation a tripartite agreement was reached between Government of India, Government of West Bengal, and Gorkha National Liberation Front on 25th July 1988 to set up an autonomous Hill Council (DGHC) under a State Act for the social, economic, educational, and cultural advancement of the people residing in the Hill areas of Darjeeling District. The Council covered the three hill subdivisions of Darjeeling district and a few Mouzas within the Siliguri sub-division.

II

This section will discuss how terror and terrorism is presented in the novel. It will elucidate both ideas and bring to fore the representation of them albeit critically.

We are first introduced to the act of terrorism in the first chapter of the novel. Sai and the judge were having tea together when the terrorists come into their house. They crept across the grass. The narrative states,

> They had come through the forest on foot, in leather jackets from the Kathmandu black market, khaki pants, bandanas—universal guerilla fashion. One of the boys carried a gun. . . . They were looking for anything they could find—kukri sickles, axes, kitchen knives, spades, any kind of firearm. They had come for the judge's hunting rifles. (4)

The fear that this terrorist attack has on the occupants of the judge's house is portrayed clearly, "The cook was hiding under the dining table and they dragged him out. "*Ai aaa, ai aa*," he joined his palms together, begging them, "please, I'm a poor man, please." He held his arms and cringed as if from an expected blow" (5). The occupants of the house feared death and did whatever that the Gorkha terrorists, who called themselves freedom fighters, forced them to do. Before they left they made their victims say "*Jai* Gorkha," "Gorkhaland for Gorkhas" (7).

Desai in her fiction states the date of the insurgency. She says: "It was February 1986. . . . In Kalimpong, high in the north eastern Himalayas where they lived—the retired judge and his cook, Sai, and Mutt—there was a report of dissatisfaction in the hills, gathering insurgency, men and guns" (9). She does not divorce the fiction from reality. The Gorkha insurgency is an integral part of Indian history. As stated in the section title Terror and Terrorism above, many lives were lost during this period. Desai depicts the reality of the time and postulates it vis-à-vis her novel with expertise. She is able to portray the fear that the terrorist act of the Gorkhas brings out in the judge's family well. The agenda of the terrorist and their attack on the judge's family is also clearly presented.

This is not the only instance of the mention of the Gorkhas intent in the novel. Desai states that when Gyan was aged 20 and Sai aged 16 they had not paid much attention to the activities going on the hills initially. People did not think that the Gorkha's demands were serious even when there were slogans scratched and painted on the sides of government offices and shops in order to show discontent (126). Until, "one day fifty boys, members of the youth wing of GNLF, gathered to swear an oath at Mahakaldara to fight to the death for the formation of a homeland, Gorkhaland. Then they marched down the streets of Darjeeling, took a turn around the market and the mall. "Gorkhaland for Gorkhas. We are the liberation army." (126). The narrative states that, "Quite suddenly, everyone was using the word insurgency" (126).

According to chapter III from a book that has been loaded on the internet that discusses the *Inheritance of Loss*:

> *The Inheritance of Loss* objectively analyses regionalism in northeastern India, especially the eighties movement for Gorkhaland. The brave, loyal and hardy Gorkhas, brought from Nepal as bonded labour and soldiers, had endured exploitation both under Britishers and in free India. Shunned by non-Nepalis, they had been denied economic, social and political rights. This injustice had been exploited by anti-state radicals, culminating in the demand for a separate state for Gorkhas led by the Gorkha National Liberation Front (GNLF). (http://shodhganga.inflibnet.ac.in/bitstream/10603/8645/10/10_chapter%203.pdf)

This fact culminates into the tragedy of the GNLF terrorism in Darjeeling, Kalimpong and other districts nearby.

The Inheritance of Loss depicts the Gorkhas asking for their rights in India. This rhetoric influences Gyan. When a man takes his audience back into history, 1947 and beyond, he tries to ignite the people's emotions and incite them. The Gorkhas are pictured to be slaves in their own country without being appreciated by the government for their efforts since they fought in World War I and World War II among other things that they have done for India, and they have worked in tea estates but they do not own them. The jobs that are advertised are not given to them since they are promised to others. Thus, Gyan thinks back to the interview that he went to in Calcutta over a year ago and remembers feeling that he will not succeed in procuring the job. Indeed he did not get the job (158-59). The above rhetoric that is depicted by Desai not only influences Gyan but others who are listening to it. Thus, the crowd becomes excited and it is stated,

> "Jai Gorkha! Jai Gorkha!" the crowd screamed, their own blood thrumming, pulsing, surging forth at the sight of the speech giver's hand. Thirty supporters stepped forward and also drew blood from their thumbs with their kukris to write a poster demanding Gorkhaland, in blood. (159)

The rhetoric mentioned in the previous paragraph is a sample of how terrorism and terrorists are created. The minds of the people are influenced and they are willing to do anything, even draw their own blood to fight for a cause that they have been made to believe in even if it is a grievous one.

Desai presents the idea of the emergence of terrorism in a very simple manner. According to the text "It just takes a few degenerate people and they drum up the illiterates, all the no-gooders hanging about with nothing to do" (201). She defines the situation accurately since the mind can be controlled with words. Those who are uneducated can be easily influenced because they do not have access to literature and their knowledge comes to them and depends only on what others tell them. As the saying goes, 'A little knowledge is dangerous."

The acts of terrorism in Kalimpong are depicted to transpire gradually. Desai states,

> Six months after Sai, Lola and Noni, Uncle Potty and Father Booty made a library trip to the Gymkhana Club, it was taken over by the Gorkha National Liberation Front, who camped out in the ballroom and the skating rink. . . . Men with guns rested in the ladies' powder room." (211)

It is also stated in the text that later evidence showed that a lot of terrorist acts were planned from this location.

This is a historical locale. It is at this place that the Gorkhas lay down their arms. According to the text, "Then when it was all over the men signed a peace treaty and moved out here at the very spot in the gymkhana Club, on these dining tables placed side by side in a row—they had staged a public surrender of arms." (212). It is stated that on 2 October 1988 during Gandhi Jayanti Day, seven thousand men surrendered together with an abundance of arms and ammunitions (212). Desai unfolds the act of terrorism that ensued in the India of 1980s vis-à-vis her novel. She transports us into the historical moment skillfully, by providing for us the exact dates of when events transpired.

However, before the end comes the people of the hills have to endure the misery that terrorism causes. The Gorkha terrorists instigated strikes in Kalimpong (235). The Gorkhas disrupted business activities in order to cause the collapse of the economy:

> Finally, the shops and offices didn't open at all—the Snow Lion Travel Agency and the STD booth, the shawl shop, the deaf tailors Kanshi Nath & Sons Newsagents—everyone terrorized to keep their shutters down and not even poke their noses out of the windows. Roadblocks stopped traffic, prevented timber and stone trucks from leaving, halted tea from being transported. Nails were scattered on the road, Mobil oil spilled all about. The GNLF boys charged large sums of money if they let you through at all and coerced you to buy GNLF speeches on cassette tapes and Gorkhaland calendars. (236)

Terrorism also affected the tourist industry in Kalimpong. Tourists stopped coming to the hills. Financially the people suffered.

The atrocities of terrorism did not end with the control of the economy. The Gorkha terrorists demanded land in exchange for peace and stability. Their demand was the "subdivisions of Darjeeling, Kalimpong, and Kurseong, and extending to the foothills, parts of Jalpaiguri and Cooch Behar districts, from Bengal into Assam" (236). To gain this they resorted to evil means and violence.

Life in Kalimpong was not safe with the Gorkha terrorists, terrorising the district. They even invade people's houses and disrupt their household like they invaded the judge's house and stole his rifles as depicted in chapter one of this novel. Another instance of such intrusion is portrayed in chapter 37. Things get out of control and the residents of Kalimpong are unable to do anything to defend themselves, their privacy and their property. They go into Lola and Noni's house who are Sai's friends. A group of them climb through the window while it's raining and start demanding food and money from the women (238). The boys do not want to leave the house and spend the night there because they believe that the police will not look for them there. This creates fear in the hearts and minds of the women. When they sleep that night they barricade their door and are insulted by the boys who say, "Don't worry. You are too old for us, you know" (239). The terrorist act has created terror in the minds and lives of the people of Kalimpong. We have to agree with Nandy who says that terrorism "is primarily a psychological weapon" (24). It "attempts to instil fear in an attempt to reach specific objectives" (24). That is what we perceive throughout the novel.

This incident does not end here. A month after the men go into their house a hut comes up on their land built by the Gorkha terrorists. When the women question them they say, "This is our land." "It is not your land. It is free land," They countered, putting down the sentence, flatly, rudely. "It is our land." "It is unoccupied land" (240). This depiction points to the fact that terrorists do not respect the rights of the people in a nation or its laws.

The terrorists do not stop harassing the people of Kalimpong. The next thing that they want to do is to burn the Indo-Nepal treaty. The terrorist went around Kalimpong from house to house demanding that the residents send at least one person from their household (272). Due to fear the people adhere to their demand. Thus, the terrorists succeed in using the psychological weapon, in this instance fear, to control the people in the Indian hills.

The burning of the documents builds up to the climax. There was a procession to the police station where the documents were to be burnt. The procession went as such, "Waving kukris, the sickle blades high and flashing in the light, "*Jai* Gorkha, " the men shouted. "*Jai* Gorkhaland! Gorkhaland for Gorkhas!" When they reached the post office it became bloody, because stones were being pelted at them. When it got out of control the police opened fire. This developed into a riot,

> In the bazaar they continued rioting. Jeeps were pushed into the ravine, buses were set on fire, the light from their burning reflected garishly on the settling mist of evening, and the fire spread to the jungles of bamboo. The air inside the hollow and stems expanded and they burst and burned with sound of renewed, magnified gunshot (277).

It did not stop here. Mass killing occurred from place to place. People could not identify their enemies. They became confused and started to question things like justice versus injustice and past versus present (295). The effects of terrorism that affected the people of Darjeeling and Kalimpong changed their lives forever. The terrorists controlled everything even the transportation service. Desai is able to show us that terrorism no matter who the perpetrators are is an evil thing. It destroys the peace and tranquillity of a nation and its people.

The Inheritance of Loss is a novel about the loss of the peace and the dignity of a nation. Aptly titled it depicts the loss of a tranquil society. The society inherits terrorism and terrorist ways because of lack of knowledge and the manipulation of those who used Machiavellian tactics to gain power and wealth. The serenity and sovereignty of the hills are lost due to those who are selfish, and want to gain power for their own means. The innocent people of the Indian hill districts suffer the effects of terrorism.

Desai's novel is only one of the many discourses that discuss the ills of terror and terrorism. There are pre 9/11 projects that have criticized terrorism. One example that has been discussed in this essay is Ashis Nandy's *The Savage Freud and Other Essays on Possible and Retrievable Selves (*1995). It outlines the terrorist agenda of the Other which in all its actuality began in the West and was labeled as such during the French Revolution. It can be concluded from his argument that terrorism is a criminal act that can cause harm to society and the world as well. Thus, we need to discuss and look into both pre and post-9/11 projects and discourses on terror and terrorism in order to understand it, what motivates its perpetrators, and how the act and its instigators can be highlighted in order to find a cure to an ill that has permeated into society.

This essay has been presented at the Transcultural Imaginaries: Making New, Making Strange Conference at the Nanyang Technological University, Singapore, 5 June 2013 with the funding from Universiti Sains Malaysia, Penang, Malaysia. Further research has been conducted in order to write and edit this essay for publication at the University of Wollongong, Sydney, New South Wales, Australia during the author's sabbatical leave from August 2013-April 2014 from which six months of that duration of time (September 2013-February 2014) have been spent at the University of Wollongong as a Visiting Fellow in order to carry out research on Malaysian, Australian and American crime fiction and theory. Universiti Sains Malaysia funded a project in 2014 on crime fiction through the grant number (1001/PHUMANITI/ 816257). Some of the research done for that project has been transferred to this paper because terrorism is also seen as a crime.

Works Cited

Desai, Kiran. *The Inheritance of Loss*, London: Penguin, 2006.

First-timer beats the odds to take Booker prize that eluded her mother. http://www.guardian.co.uk/uk/2006/oct/11/books.bookerprize2006

Kamal, Muhammad. The Meaning of Terrorism: A Philosophical Inquiry. *NCEIS Research Papers,* 1, 1 (2008), 1-11.

Krueger, Alan B. *What Makes a Terrorist,* Princeton: Princeton University Press, 2002.

Laushey, David M. *Bengal Terrorism and the Marxist Left,* Calcutta: Firma K.L. Mukhophadyay, 1975.

Merriam-Webster. http://www.merriam-webster.com/dictionary/terror

Mishra, Pankaj. Wounded by the West, *The New York Times*, 12 February 2006. http://www.nytimes.com/2006/02/12/books/review/ 12mishra. html? pagewanted=all&_r=0 (2006).

Mohamed Ali, Halimah, *Orientalism from within: A Critical Study of Pandering and Catering to the West in Three Contemporary In-*

dian-English Novels. (Unpublished Doctoral Thesis, 2006). Universiti Kebangsaan Malaysia, Bangi.

_____. *Orientalism from within: Arundhati Roy and Her Contemporaries.* Pulau Pinang: Universiti Sains Malaysia. 2011.

Nandy, Ashis. *The Savage Freud and Other Essays on Possible and Retrievable Selves,* Princeton: Princeton University Press. (1995).

Sabharwal, Gopa. *The Indian Millennium AD 1000-2000,* New Delhi: Penguin, 2000.

Setty, Sudha. What's in a name? How nations define terrorism ten years after 9/11. *U. Pa. J. Int'l L.* 33, 1 (2011), 1-63.

Singh, Shiv Sahay. Gorkhaland demand still alive. http://www.the hindu.com/news/states/other-states/article3727023.ece. (2012).

Tamang, Munish, Prasingh, Bharatiya. Gorkha. *A Very Short Introduction to the History and Issues of Gorkhaland.* http://www. darjeelingtimes.com/main-news/98-citizen-news/4126-the-history-and -issues- of-gorkhaland.html. (2013)

Binary Identities and Contesting Cultures in Kiran Desai's *The Inheritance of Loss*

SERWANI V. SWAMY
Anil Neerukonda Instt. of Tech. and Sc., Visakhapatnam

During colonial phase, the immigrants in England were at the mercy and under subjugation of the English hegemony. The marginal treatment left the immigrants with a fractured identity. Since the 1970s, global movements exposing multi-culture, transcending multiple identities and cultural adaptations is seen. The identities in such conditions are in motion and fluctuating. In the context of dislocations the identities are hardly stabilized and presumably fragmented and fluid. The Indian immigrants are coloured immigrants in the elite multinational countries. The interconnectivity of cultures encourages ideas and traditions from one culture and blends them with the others. The immigrants encounter various cultural challenges in the adopted land and are subjected to reclusion and solitude in the dominant host culture. This is characterized by their admiration of the host culture which they consider superior to their own ethnic culture. It is a mixed culture which is a blend of both the cultures: one of the native root culture and the other the host culture creating a 'third culture' different from their own. This paper articulates 'Hybridity' as a cultural camouflage, explored in the Man Booker Prize winning novel *The Inheritance of Loss* by Kiran Desai. The characters are exposed to issues of immigration, cultural conflicts, and identity flux, struggling to make place in the alien country. In the fundamental transnational movements, the instability of the characters represents living in in-between spaces which is termed by Bhabha as 'threshold' in *The Location of Culture*. It propels the immigrants on two planes of the boundary towards nowhereness.

Kiran Desai's novel is set partly in India and partly in the U.S.A. and in England. She captures the immigration experiences and also the Indian native environment. *The Inheritance of Loss* is a novel of crossing over boundaries to, two major multinational countries, one to England in 1935 and another to America in the 1980s. She manages to fathom internal struggles in independent India as well as the immigrant struggle in multinational countries. She uncovers the anguish felt by the Gorkha community, a struggle for self-identity and striving for empowerment in postcolonial scenario. She blends these issues with embittered human illegal immigration. The novel portrays the predicament of immigration like cultural contradictions, alienation, hybridity and mimicry, reflecting postcolonial period.

The significant challenges emerge in context of changing borders in a specific time and place. The protagonist Jemubhai Patel's immigration takes place in the pre-independence period in 1935, in pursuit of education, whereas Biju's immigration marks the moment of canonical upsurge of global movements in the 1980s for economic gain, celebration and social elevation. Jemubhai Patel and Biju's identity is influenced by admiration for the English as a result of empowering colonialism. The former's admiration withdraws him into a cocoon and masked identity whereas the latter is candid in his desire to live like English 'angrez ki tarah' (105). The yearning to immigrate regardless of class and community is what Bhabha defines as the imitation of the British, "Setting in the 1970s to study English at Oxford was, in many ways, culmination of an Indian middleclass trajectory where formal education and 'high' culture colluded in emulating the canons of elite 'English' taste . . . and conforming to its customs and comforts" (x). Jemubhai's immigration to England for Cambridge education indicates the upsurge in changing education system, aspiring for graduating in England which is considered as a celebration and a matter of pride in Indian communities. It is the outcome of "the infamous Macaulay Minute of February 2, 1835 declared the superiority of the colonial education over the native education" (qtd. Chatterjee 166-83), which gave supremacy and a preference to English education than to native education in India. Jemubhai an anglophile is one such colonial immigrant undoubtedly a follower of the colonizers. His father, Boman Bhai Patel's main aim is to send him to England, at any cost and make him an ICS, which holds him an honourable position in his community. He alienates himself from his nativity and encounters cultural and racial challenges. This fluctuating dual culture makes him a 'hybrid,' a mind of fractured psyche.

The term hybridity in *The Location of Culture* is one of Bhabha's most significant concepts; it creates space for both the host and the exile culture. According to Bhabha, it marks the space of ambivalence theory in the context of cultural identity. Edward Said, a self-exile to the U.S., has always associated himself with Palestinian movement for liberation and sovereign state. His views on culture and creativity are different. In an interview with Salman Rushdie (Said 1995) he says, "The whole notion of crossing over or moving from one identity to another is extremely important to me. Being as I am as we all are a sort of hybrid" as (qtd. Singh 22). Here, Said generalizes the term 'hybridity' and emphasizes the change of identity as diaspora and terms it as 'crossing over.' It traditionally connotes of being 'impure,' in the postcolonial context. It delves in living in the cultural duality in in-betweenness. Kraidy shows that Bhabha explores "hybridity in the context of the postcolonial novel and celebrates it as a symptom of resistance by the colonized, as the contamination of imperial ideology, aesthetics and identity by natives striking back at colonial domination." (qtd. 530). According to Bhabha, the subject of the hybridity is the mocking of the colonial dominance.

Delineating Bhabhas's concept, scholars like Robert Young (1995) and Stuart Hall (1992) gave remarkable definition of hybridity, however Bhabha's definition has been the most specific and prominent. Bhabha observes that hybridity is the problem of colonial empowerment, between the white presence and black semblance and it is definitely not uniting colonizer and colonized. It creates mimic men precariously place in in-between spaces. The term 'mimicry' is a process of 'hybridization.' It produces dual identity which is different than their original, a camouflaged reflection of the English. The change according to Ashcroft is, "a means of evading the replication of the binary categories of the past and developing new anti-monolithic models of cultural exchange and growth" (qtd. Rahaman 3). Jemubhai, Sai, Lola and Noni are conscious of mixed hybrid identities. Jemubhai is apparently unsettled in his own culture as much as in the alien culture. It places him in ambivalence as belonging to nowhere. This psychological nowhereness is termed by Uma Parmeswaran as 'Trishanku,' (*Trishanku and Other Writings* 1998). She links it to mythological perception: she refers it to the myth of a king who lived between heaven and earth, who doesn't belong to any of the two. The immigrants' condition resembles that of Trishanku, a state of in-betweenness.

Jemubhai and Biju are two cracked identities facing duality, distancing them from ethnic identity. Jemubhai's typical dark skin, language and his attire are a reminder of his Third World origins. He is discriminately alienated and humiliated by the white Europeans to prove their superiority. In 1942 Jemubhai, as a young man encounters acidic treatment by the officials. When taking open competitive examination at Cambridge in England, he recites a poem of Sir Walter Scott in his native accent and to his embarrassment, "When he looked up, he saw they were all chuckling" (113). The humiliation infused so badly that when he interviews Gyan years after in India for a tutor's post, the sour memories haunt him, "envelope him in its nightmare" (113). His failing emotion engulfs him and transforms him into inferiorly unapproachable person, withdrawn into a shell of loneliness:

> Thus it was that the judge eventually took revenge on his early confusion, his embarrassment gloved in something called 'keeping up standards,' his accent behind mask of a quiet. He found he began to be mistaken for something he wasn't—a man of dignity. This accidental poise became more important than any other thing. He envied the English. He loathed the Indians. He worked at being English with the passion of hatred and for what he would become, he would be despised by absolutely everyone, English and Indians, both (119).

His education in England causes him so much hurt and agony that he desperately tries to become as English as possible, and callous to anything Indian, including his family and wife.

Jemubhai Patel's granddaughter Sai, brought up in Russia, is another example of hybridity. She becomes an anglophile, influenced by her dominant alien environment from a very young age and her anglicized convent education in India. Biju, the cook's son is another immigrant who fancies, celebration of immigration desires to become an English gentleman and expresses immigration to America as elevation of his status in his society. Biju imitates the hybrid culture, becomes critical of his native culture and admires the white skin of Americans, he says: "white people looked clean because they are white the darker you were, the dirtier you looked" (186). However, his immigration to America transforms him and makes him critical of the alien culture. He sways between the two cultures but is strong enough to hold on to his religious beliefs: "One should not give up one's religion. . . . No, matter what" (136).

There is evident contrasting class difference between nativity and hybridity. Sai who is from a decent and Western upbringing celebrates Christmas, eats western food and apes Western culture. This association to alien culture irritates Gyan, a Gorkha minority. He accuses her of copying the English."Why do you celebrate Christmas? You're Hindus and you don't celebrate Id or Guru Nanak's Birthday or even Durga Puja or Dussehra or Tibetin New Year. . . . You are like slaves, that's what you are, running after the west, embarrassing yourself. It's because of people like you we never get anywhere (63).

Similarly Lola and Noni, anglophile Bengali, sisters, lure for the Western culture and celebrate Christmas along with father Booty and uncle Potty. Bhabha in *Of Mimicry and Man: The Ambivalence of Colonial Discourse, analyses that* at the intersection of European learning and colonial power, *Macaulay* can conceive of nothing other than "a class of interpreters between us and the millions whom we govern-a class of persons Indian in blood and colour, but English in tastes, in opinions, in morals and in intellect" (qtd. in Bhabha128). He further says Mimic men are raised through the influence of English schools in India. Sai's argument to have her own way of lifestyle, illustrates her inclination towards the 'other' alien culture. The unconscious influence of her early immigration, entirely anglicized St. Augustine's convent environment school at Dehradun's and her anglicized grandfather, have sown the seeds of hybrid culture. Moreover she associates with her neighbours who have a fascination for Western culture.

Gyan reflects a torn identity and sways between Western identity and native Nepali identity. The cultural barriers and the frustrations distance him from Sai though he loves her. She flinches when she visits his house, "The house did not match Gyan's talk, his English, his books, his clothes, or his schooling. It didn't match his future. . . . She felt shame, then for him. How he must have hoped his silence would be construed as dignity" (256). She feels distaste of herself and wonders how she got linked to this predicament without her knowledge. For Sai, rejection was heartbreaking but she makes her point clear, "You hate me," said Sai "for big reasons, that have nothing to do with me. You aren't being fair." (260). When Gyan, finds his ethnic roots he turns against the Western culture or hybrid culture, which dominates persons like Sai and her grandfather who have lost their originality. Gyan detests their adapting to Western culture and says that they are *copycats* who admire culture of the Americans who in fact do not desire them. "THEY DON'T WANT YOU!!!!" (164).

Gyan's ethnic loyalty comes between choosing Sai and his community, who prefers the latter, eliminating Sai from his life. To defend his guilt conscious, he targets her hybridity as the reason for his betrayal of her. Gyan critically sneers her culture that she is fluent in English rather than in Hindi. She could not eat with her hands and squat on floor as any Indian. She has never been to temple except for architectural interest, nor has relished native sweets and films. Bollywood films exhausted her, but felt happy with English movies and food. Her hybrid culture always made him inferior. Hence he exposes her inability to adapt to her 'other culture' which is the native culture:

> Eating together they had always felt embarrassed—he unsettled by her finickiness and her curbed enjoyment, and she revolted by his energy and his fingers working the dal, his slurps and smacks. The judge ate even his chapatis, his puris and parathas, with knife and fork. Insisted that Sai, in his presence, do the same (176).

The duplicity lands her in a stage of in-betweenness and the question of her identity lingers on her mind. Sai's neighbours, her first tutor Noni, the spinster who lives with her widowed sister, Lola have affiliation to western culture. They have a high regard for the British English books which reflect the identity of multicultural, Westernized society. They disrespect the colonial reference in V.S. Naipaul's *A Bend in the River*, "uphill task" (46). Lola expresses her disappointment on the colonial impact in the novel, "I think he's strange. Stuck in the past. . . . He has not progressed. Colonial neurosis, he's never freed himself from it" (46). Lola criticizes that Naipaul lives in the past, when they are into advanced multicultural and globalization period. She states how the culture has been revolutionizing, "chicken tikka masala has replaced fish and chips as the No. 1 take-out dinner in Britain" (46). The sisters not only follow the culture and mannerism but also follow the foreign brands: "Her suitcases were stuffed with Marmite, Oxo bouillon cubes, Knorr soup packets, After Eights, daffodil bulbs, and renewed supplies of boots cucumber lotion, and Marks and Spenser underwear—the essence, quintessence of Englishness as she understood it. Surely the queen donned this superior hosiery" (46-47). Lola also boasts of her daughter Pixie being highly acclaimed BBC news reporter with British accent and swank of English plays, strawberries and cream etc. They prefer whatever is British or American rather than Indian. Her daughter, a mimic of the British, speaks her name in English accent "This is Piyali Banerjee with the BBC" to the amazed and amusing ears of Indians. Desai brings out the humour of imitation and mockery of fluctuating identities. Adriana Elena Stoican puts in, "The sisters' consumption habits as well as their cultural preferences indicate the elitist dimension of their Western practices" (n.pag). Mrs. Sen, another admirer of America, boasts of her daughter:

> Oh they keep begging her to take a green card, she says, 'No, no, I told her what is there? If they're *offering* it, pushing it on you. . . .' How many people will kill for one? . . . Silly goose, isn't it so? What a bee-oo-teeful country and so well organized (131).

The characters marvel the hybrid culture and hunger for Western identities, demeaning Indian culture. For such hybridity people '*the grass is greener on the other side.*' It reflects the hollowness of identities in scarching for foreign culture leaving behind ethnic and own culture. Gyan's community shows a camouflaged hybrid identity. The Gorkhas, the "unleashed Brucelee fans in their American T-shirts made in China-coming-in-via-Kathmandu?" (157), are ironically transforming and shaping into hybrid form. Gyan a cynic often wishes to line at the American embassy or the British to leave the native country, as he once suggests Sai "lets fly to Australia" (157) that would give him freedom of history free from family demands and debts of centuries. His identity is ambivalence like Biju who wants to be free from historical bondage and desires a path, where he can survive in dignity and be part of globalization. The cook also marvels hybrid culture, anything foreign is important other than their own country. He even feels low-grade to work under an India officer whereupon he glorifies his father who worked for English men."The cook had been disappointed to be working for Jemubhai, a severe comedown, he thought because his father, who served white men only. The ICS was becoming Indianized and they didn't like it" (63). His petty earnings at the judge's house do not stop him from boasting his son's immigration to American. "My son works in New York . . . very big city, the cars and buildings are nothing like here. In that country, there is enough food for everybody" (84).

In such colonial encounter and global immigration, the identity is bound to be hybrid. Salman Rushdie observes in *East, West* that no culture is unaffected by another culture in today's postcolonial world and attains only single identity. As Bhabha says: a different culture, "neither the One . . . nor the other . . . but something else besides" (*Commitment* 4). Characters like Jemubhai, Sai and Biju resemble colonial products and represent hybridity and bewildered cultural duality. Jemubhai is subjected to ambivalence in 'masked' culture which he cannot imbibe and the native culture which is below his recognition. He satisfies his internal psyche, lives in a French house and accepts his granddaughter only because she reflects hybrid culture. He looks after a dog which shows his elite culture. He deserts his wife and despises her for her inability to match his culture. He undergoes cultural transformation and displays a hybrid, binary identity, belonging to a space which is in-betweenness.

The immigrants experience the 'other alien culture' and are unable to escape the dominance of its influence. The characters face cultural conflicts and identity flux struggling to sustain the prominent global cultural change. Adaptability of the alien culture drives them to attain a 'third culture' which is neither completely their own, nor the native root culture. The culture that is attained is hybrid mixed culture which is *de facto* a transformation process essentially irreversible.

Works Cited

Bhabha, Homi K. The Location of Culture. New York &London: Routledge, 1994.

_____, "Of Mimicry and Man: The Ambivalence of Colonial Discourse" October, Vol. 28 (1984):125-33.

Chatterjee, Purnendu."The Inheritance of Loss: Mapping Postcolonial Indian masculinities" *Postcolonial Indian Fiction in English and Masculinity*, ed. Mittapalli, Rajeshwar and Letizia Alterno. New Delhi: Atlantic, 2009, xiv, 226.166-83.

Desai, Kiran. *The Inheritance of Loss.* New York: Atlantic, 2006.

Kraidy, M. Marwin. *Hybridity, OR the Cultural Logic of Globalization* New Delhi Temple University Press, 2005.

Parmeswaran, Uma. "Home is where your feet are, and make your heart be there!" *Writers of Indian Diaspora: Theory and Practice* Ed. Jasbir Jain Rawat Publication, 1996. 30-39

Singh, Gurbhagat. "Expatriate Writing and the problematic of the Centre: Edward Said and Homi Bhabha" *Writers of Indian Diaspora; Theory and Practice*, ed. Jasbir Jain New Delhi: Rawat, 1998,

Stoican, Adriana Elena. "Competing hegemonies in Kiran Desai's *The Inheritance of Loss*," *Humanicus*:7 (2012): n.p.

Rushdie, Salman."At the auction of the Ruby Slippers." *East West*. London: Vintage, 1994. 85-105.

Valiur, Rahaman "Liminality, Mimicry, Hybridity and Ambivalent Literary Speculations of Homi K. Bhabha," *Homi Bhabha's Literary Theory*, Germany: GRIN Verlag, 2010.

A Feminist Approach to Arundhati Roy's *The God of Small Things*

RAKESH YADAV
Res. Sch., Lalit Narayan Mithila University

Feminists identify the deep-rooted causes leading to oppression of women and an endeavor to remove them. They try to bring about a change in the social milieu in which women are accepted as equals, in all respects to men in the equal sharing of rights, opportunities and responsibilities in the process of evolution of human society. Some restrict their demands to equality in matters relating to education and work with emphasis on financial independence. There are others, among the feminists, who call for a metamorphosis of the entire society with a view to completely removing the tradition-bound, deep-rooted beliefs in the moral superiority of man over woman. Their purpose is to eradicate the persisting gender discrimination in all its manifestations in the society.

There is, however, some change in the attitude of the woman herself as an individual in her own right. It is in this context that Indian women writers like Anita Desai, Shashi Deshpande, Kamala Markandaya, Arundhati Roy and Jhumpa Lahiri, to name only a few, depict the anxiety of the educated, independent, middle-class Indian woman searching for a balance between her traditional role as daughter, wife and mother in a predominantly patriarchal society and her new-found sense of self-longing freedom and private space. Slowly becoming aware of the injustice heaped on them, women began to raise their voice in protest and this led to the birth of Women's Liberation Movement in the early nineteen seventies.

Elite women living in major cities were initially drawn into the vortex of the feminist movement and their main role was to bring home to the women of diverse sections of society, how they were subjected to iniquitous and humiliating treatment in this custom-bound male dominated environment. With the passage of time, more and more votaries of feminism joined the ranks of the movement.

Indian woman's identity is one that is usually connected to and defined by societal and cultural norms of a patriarchal familial structure. Her identity is defined within the parameters of her social relationship to man. The Indian woman is a metaphor for purity, chastity and sanctity of the ancient spirit that is Indian. This essential spirit of India lies in its religion, spirituality, culture, tradition and family.

Arundhati Roy arrived as a public figure on the larger Indian literary stage like some dramatic unforeseen comet. John Updike compared Roy's arrival in fiction to that of Tiger Woods in golf. Commenting upon the unique success of Arundhati Roy as novelist of *The God of Small Things* at a very young age, Kamala Das says, "She is lucky. We are not. But she is our child and we wish her well. We are very happy for her. Because she is young to enjoy it." The novel is about love and hate, body and sex, marriage and divorce, conflict and struggle and, above all, it is about women. "We're prisoners of war. . . . Our dreams have been doctored. We belong nowhere. We sail unanchored on troubled seas. We may never be allowed ashore. Our sorrows will never be said enough. Our joys never happy enough. Our dream never big enough. Our lives never important enough."[3] The above lines said by Chacko are well matched and symbolically fit for the women characters of the novel—Baby Kochamma, Mammachi, Ammu and Rahel. Roy's concept of feminism can be examined by the way the women characters faced crisis and how they reacted with dilemma and obstacles in the novel.

In this paper, I will try to establish the fact that Roy has introduced some revolutionary approach while writing this novel and her treatment of women characters. The novel is a tale of three generations of women. It displays the struggle of the women against their incessant exploitation, torture and struggle which they face in the male-dominated conservative society. "It can be called the story of sufferings of Baby Kochamma, Mammachi, Ammu and Rahel. They all suffer in different ways. In a country like India where patriarchal system is very strong, women suffer mentally, physically and sexually."[4]

The novel deals with the confrontation between the Haves and Have-Nots of the society, between the High and the Mighty, and the Low and the Weak, "Big man, The Laltain and the Small, the Mombati, between the god of big things and the god of small things."

Roy also presents a deep contrast between man and woman. For centuries man has been dominating over the family and society, as also the woman. The life-course, action and mission of woman is controlled and guided by man. Symbolically, to some extent, man is Laltain and woman is Mombati. While man, i.e. Laltain is strong, powerful, protected and has full freedom, woman is still lingering on the will of man. In the novel, Ammu and Chacko are brother and sister. But Ammu is not allowed to get proper education and go abroad while Chacko goes to Oxford. After the divorce of Ammu, she is not welcomed by her parents. However, Chacko is warmly received by the family after the divorce from an English woman, Margaret. He is always trying to show his manhood and throwing his weight around. He boastfully tells his sister: "What is yours is mine and what is mine is also mine." (58)

Pappachi, father of Ammu, was a frustrated man. After his retirement, he was a changed man—ill-tempered and difficult to adjust with. Once again, dominance over woman by man is shown in the character of Pappachi. He used to beat his wife with brass flower vase violently. He was a monster for his own family—a Laltain, a man for a woman, Ammu and Mammachi, Mombattis before him.

Chacko came back to Ayemenem, started "Paradise Pickles and Preserves" keeping his mother a neutral partner and at last hijacked all parental wealth, house and factory under him. So, he is a true representative of "wonderful male chauvinistic society."

How shocking and disgusting that Ammu's husband forces her to have sex with his boss, Mr. Hollick, to save his job. Ammu revolted against the so-called dogmatic foundation of the society. She married a Bengali going against her conservative parents; she challenged the supremacy and authority of her brother, Chacko. She dared to take divorce from her husband and left him. Roy tries to give a stern message to Indian women to challenge the bad custom or tradition that is harming their lives and follow their own way of lives and decide the course of lives.

Marriage is considered a pious and important aspect in the life of Indian woman. She enters into marriage easily but it is not easy to come out from the marriage if it fails. Here once again Roy's women characters prove themselves ultramodern and revolutionary. Ammu and her daughter Rahel realized after a short while that their marriage was just a tragic disaster. "Rahel drifted into marriage like a passenger drifts towards an unoccupied chair in an airport longue" (17)

Both Ammu and Rahel took a very bold decision. They broke their marriage and came out from this so-called social and pious bond-marriage. They wanted to live their lives as per their choice. "Anything that makes you weak physically, intellectually and spiritually, reject as poison."[5]

But the most promising quality of Roy's women is their will power and choice of love-life or love partner. Baby Kochamma, when she was young, fell in love with a handsome Irish monk,

Father Mulligan. She was so much attracted to him that she tried all means to seduce him. She even converted to Roman Catholic against the wishes of her father. She entered a convent in Madras as a trainee nun to come close to Father but in vain. But she did not marry in her later life. Instead she used to write "I love you! I love you" in her personal diary. She felt that "her memory of him was hers. Wholly hers. Savagely, fiercely hers. Not to be shared with faith, far less with competing, co-nuns, and co-sadhus or whatever it was they called themselves." (286)

One main reason of weakness of woman is her financial dependence on man. Mammachi, in spite of her husband's objection, started "Paradise Pickles and Preserves," a small pickle factory, in her own house. Ammu worked in her mother's factory as a worker and later she went to the Bharat Lodge in Alleppey for a job interview for the post of secretary. Rahel, daughter of Ammu, worked as a waitress in an Indian restaurant in New York. She also worked as a night clerk in a bullet proof cabin at a gas station outside Washington.

Roy has been severely criticized for her portrayal of sexual aspects which look absurd and they could have been easily done away with. But she wants to show emphatically that woman should have the same right as man even to choose the life or sex partner. Ammu is a brave woman who challenges the social order by marrying a person of her choice and then breaking that marriage and getting entangled in a forbidden love affair with Velutha who was an untouchable and a paravan in Kerala society. A common reader may object to her decision to have love and sex with Velutha. But Roy has given such freedom to her woman to select and decide her partner: "We will not allow our bodies to be owned and controlled by men in government or men anywhere for that matter. We will not allow our compassionate souls to get stepped on."[6]

Roy's fictional art is remarkable for the innovations in language. Her language embellishes, communicates and strives for visionary effects. She uses Indian brand of English that deviates from the standard convention. She uses Malayalam words, phrases, sentences and accent. She uses many Malayalam words to give a south Indian touch to the writing. For example,

Malayalam word	English meaning
*Chichi poach	Shit-wiper
*Mundu	Dhoti
*Onner, runder, mooner	One, two, three
*Velutha	White
*Naaley	Tomorrow

Roy takes up classic Indian materials but delights in verbal innovation and linguistic experiment. It is indeed a bold step for woman writer who is writing her first novel. She has stretched language and imagination to recreate the fun-filled, magical yet anguished world of childhood with poignant simplicity.

Roy is a feminist novelist whose maiden novel was highly praised. Her women characters are ultra-modern and dynamic. They dare to break their marriage as per their will and love the person whom they like, breaking the bondage of society. They have the courage to challenge man's supremacy over woman by protesting against parents and male members of the family. They try to come out of the shadow of man by becoming economically independent. As Rushdie says: "I think it's an important landmark which cannot be overlooked, not only because it brings home a Booker but also because it records Mombattis' brave though unfortunate struggle to survive against crazy winds of caste, class, and gender in independent India."[7]

NOTES

1. The Bristol Woman's Studies Group, ed. "Half the Sky: An Introduction to Women's Studies (London: Virgo) 1979. P-39.

2. Dushyant B. Nimavat, "Theme of Suffering and Exploitation in Arundhati Roy's *The God of Small Things* and Toni Morrison's Novel," Atlantic, 2001, 142.
3. Arundhati Roy, *The God of Small Things*. Penguin
4. Rashmi Singh, "Feminist Movement of the Nineties with Special Reference to Arundhati Roy's *The God of Small Things*." Unpublished U.G.C Project, 2002
5. risikajain.com/2014/01/11top-ten-famous-quotes-of-swami-vivekananda
6. Alicia Keys (Singer), qtd. *The Times of India*, 23 January, 2017.
7. Salman Rushdie, "Interview," *The New Yorker*. June 30.1997.

Marital Relations: The Novels of Anita Desai, Bharati Mukherjee and Shashi Deshpande

M. SRILAKSHMI
D.V.R. & Dr. H.S. MIC College of Tech., Kanchikacherla

The Indian society has the highly hierarchical nature of family and the concept of equality is quiet unknown to women. The intimate personal experiences and psychological habits in India tend to be dominated by conventional mores and traditional experiences where even the constitutional guarantee of equality to women is superseded by social institutions like marriage and religion. As such the concept of alienation is projected mainly through marital relationships. In the Indian cultural context, marriage, an important institution, links to it the lives of the protagonists, except a few. From the point of women marriage is not a mere sociological institution, but a personal experience with love and understanding.

Literature, besides reflecting social reality fashions the intricate ways in which men and women manage themselves, their marital relationships and their perception of the socio-cultural reality. Indian women novelists have dealt with marriage with high seriousness because the tradition of India gives great importance to it. They have extensively dealt with the theme of marriage which has an immense sociological, historical and cultural significance. Sufferings of Indian women after marriage, marital disharmony, existentialism, anger, dual tradition are the major themes of feminist writing. The institution of marriage which leads to the quest for identity of the protagonists has been the centre of attraction for writers like Anita Desai, Shashi

Deshpande and Bharati Mukherjee. Anita Desai has added a new dimension to the achievement of Indian women writers in English fiction. Shashi Deshpande focuses on the problems of working women. Bharati Mukherjee like her Western counterparts discusses the moral dilemma that women face.

In Anita Desai the quest for a true self is sparked by a crisis which leads to the immediate past which is highly dominated by marriage and marital relations. While Toto's death gives Maya a chance to ponder over her marriage which is marked by lack of understanding and communication, fifth pregnancy forces Sita to evaluate her marital relationship. The marriages of both Maya and Sita are born out of convenience and the partners drift away failing to hold on to each other for emotional rapport. The prospect of loneliness in them is as disturbing as that of being trapped in a loveless marriage. Anita Desai's women constantly battle with boredom, inertia and ennui. The relationship of Maya, a sensitive wife and Gautama, a prosaic husband, is imprinted by silence as it fails to achieve a harmony of understanding between them. An ever-widening gap in communication between the husband and wife is sensed throughout the novel. Restlessness always boils within her and the silence holds them apart. She always feels defenseless and utterly alone in the company of her husband who ignored her sensitive feelings. From an ordinary pampered hypersensitive child-bride, Maya is transformed within four years of married life into a mere neurotic, homicidal maniac in the attempt to compromise with her marriage, which was destined to fail, right from the beginning. Homogeneity of interests and attitudes is conducive to a happy marriage. But in this marriage the rational and matter of fact world of Gautama clashes with the sentimental and emotional world of Maya. In Maya's marriage it is not compatibility and love, but silence, lack of understanding and obligations that gain prominence. Sita and Raman too lack understanding and proper communication. People who live under the same roof without sharing the essential communion of hearts become strangers. This is what makes Sita and Raman strangers. There is no coordination between Sita and Raman. Sita is sensitive and emotional while Raman is cold and indifferent. Raman is depicted neither as an introvert nor an extrovert but as a meddling kind of man. Like Gautama, in *Cry the Peacock,* he is intelligent, sane, and rationale but lacks empathy to understand his wife's temperament. Even there is no fully eventuated adult love between Raman and Sita.

A harmony in lives is what the protagonists of Desai fail to achieve in their desire to love and live clashes with the world of reality. Lack of this they are permanently in quest of a more pure existence than that is available to them. Besides, they lack surrender and involvement. Unlike Maya, Sita tries to achieve peace of mind by alienating from others. It is lack of communication between the spouses that leads to failure in both the matrimonial relationships. The impossibility of verbal communication with the spouses causes Maya and Sita to withdraw to a world of silence. The protagonists who occasionally indulge in introspection lack the courage and maturity to achieve an honest self appraisal. Various attempts to escape their cages make them mentally bruised and spiritually battered. Their worlds become destructive with their near neurotic urges, lonely strivings and desperation. When the demands on the self become unbearable they either withdraw or choose homicide or suicide or murder as a solution to their problems. In *Cry, the Peacock*, Maya's solipsism ends in brutal killing of her husband whom she finds incapable of living. In *Where Shall We Go This Summer?* Sita withdraws into silence, leaves to the island of Manori, finally compromises and returns to Bombay.

Mukherjee's Dimple and Jasmine vary in their views regarding marriage. For Jasmine marriage is not an absolute goal as it is for Dimple. For the ever-accommodating and many-married Jasmine, each marriage designs a different destiny for her, none of which is dissatisfying. Each marriage helps her to trek towards establishing her own identity. She fights through various situations in her flight to succeed. Marriage provides her a sense of fulfillment than it does to Dimple. Towards the end we find a marked change in Jasmine's attitude towards marriage. The girl, who murdered Half-Face for violating her chastity without marrying, now willingly chooses not only to live with an American as wife (with a new identity Jane Ripplemeyer) without being married to him but carries his child in her womb also.

Desai's *Cry, the Peacock* and Mukherjee's *Wife* explore the innermost feelings of neurotic individuals. Dimple, like Maya, undergoes an intense sense of loneliness and gets mentally disturbed. Dimple becomes the victim of a career-oriented husband and Maya of an older man who has no feelings and time for her. Both the protagonists are lonely. There exist many similarities between the two protagonists like the stages of disenchantment with respect to their situation in life, dissatisfaction and the onset of mental disturbance. These similarities augment the mental tension and make them insane. Dimple like Maya fails to communicate with the people around her and even with her own self. Dimple's initial dream of marriage, freedom, love and luxury life contradict with what she really attains. Amit and the husband of her fantasy totally contradict with each other. In mere obsession she measures her husband against her dream man and her own life against her dream. America, which she imagines to be the land of freedom, shocks her as she realizes that it doesn't make Indian women free but only gives little escape. She views both Love and Death as the most important things just as Maya of Anita Desai's *Cry, the Peacock.* For Maya it is the dance of the peacock and for Dimple it is America that stands for love and death. It is Gautama's inability to comfort the troubled psyche that leads to the tragic predicament of Maya and it is cultural transplantation and obsession to the world of fantasy that cripples the mind of Dimple. While Gautama never tries rescue Maya of her horrifying nightmares, Amit hampers Dimple's attempts to fulfill her dreams. Dimple's husband's restrictions do not allow her free movement in America and suppress her desire to follow the trends of the American society. This influences her psyche a lot as she had married Amit and accompanied him to America only with the intention of attaining liberation from the limitations of the middle-class life in India. Disappointed with life for various reasons both the protagonists become neurotic and slowly descent to the role of murderers. Maya's act of murdering her husband and Dimple's killing of her husband are acts of self-liberation.

Unlike the maladjusted marriages born out of convenience which make the wives miserable or neurotics in Desai and Mukherjee, the love marriages of Deshpande's protagonists confer on them only split-personalities. Deshpande's novels usually begin with an unorthodox marriage leading to the problems of alienation, accommodation and adjustment. The conflict in her protagonists is resolved through their desperate unconscious submission to traditional roles. Thus, despite the impact of western culture and alien mores and values on them, they remain intrinsically Indian in sensibility. Their deviation from a traditional way of life is just a detour. Torn between the awareness of the need for establishing their individuality and the demands on them by the cultural constraints, they become schizophrenics. Marriage proves to be another trap where Saru and Indu feel like caged animals. Making enormous sacrifices on their profession, the protagonists begin to understand that marriage obstructs their growth as individuals. They see marriage only in terms of the dark rooms where terror awaits them. It looks as if they had exchanged one pair of pinching, torturing shoes for another. Marriage doesn't bring change in their lives as they have to walk carefully on the chalked lines drawn by others. In this process one step this side or that ruins their lives.

Like Desai novels, each Deshpande novel also begins with a crisis in marriage that provides scope for introspection: for Saru it is the nightly assaults by her husband and for Indu dissatisfaction with work. Through the landscape of their minds Deshpande addresses the issues concerning the individuality of women. Marriage forces Deshpande women to mask their real selves. Even the liberated and educated Indu is compelled to be passive and unresponsive, carefully hiding her real self from Jayant who remains a conventional husband expecting his wife to play a submissive role. Indu is discouraged as a writer by her husband. Saru-Manu marriage turns sour because of sexual sadism emanating from professional jealousy. The professional growth of Saru gradually weakens Manu which he tries to overcome by sexual assaults.

The protagonists of all the three authors except Jasmine fail to communicate and resort to silence. Each of these marriages is marked by silence. As liberation is speaking out and making contact, silence is oppression. Whether it is Maya, Sita, Indu, Saru or Dimple the silence that creeps into all these women is symptomatic of alienation, apprehension and anger rooted in different forms: a silence which is often misunderstood by men as the symbol of contentment. Most of the relationships, according to Deshpande, wither and totter due to silence. The role of a submissive wife makes Indu dissatisfied and silent. Indu's husband Jayant believes that passion makes a woman unwomanly and expects Indu to be submissive even in the sexual act. This silence causes a rift between Indu and Jayant. Silence is a complex dynamic affecting Saru's relationships with her husband and there is no exaggeration in saying that all major and minor problems are due to lack of communication. All confusion and chaos in Saru's life might have resolved if she had tried to come out of her silence by talking to her husband.

In one form or another, the theme of marriage dominates the contemporary fiction. It is one of the central themes in the works Anita Desai, Shashi Deshpande and Bharati Mukherjee. The protagonists in their married lives fail to establish good interpersonal relationships due to uncongenial domestic environments characterized by emotional deprivation and lack of understanding. Also childhood influences like parental neglect or partiality, gender discrimination and lack of peer group or sibling support influence them. Sexual abuse, loneliness, despair, identity crisis, thwarting of individuality, dislocation and culture shock to contribute to darken the married lives of these protagonists. The portrayal of such characters not only exhibits the psychological insight of the novelists but also suggests the need for harmony between the inner world and external realities which gives a happy ending to their married lives. These novelists present life as it is and emphasize that the liberation must come from within. They advocate that harmony in married life can be achieved by change of mind, breaking silence, gaining positive recognition and learning to assimilate without surrendering individuality. Finally, a world devoid of cramping childhood experiences, gender discrimination, sexual abuse, identity crisis, thwarting of individuality, dislocation, incompatible relations ensures unsullied dignity and individuality to women enabling her to emerge out of the problems and lead a happy married life.

Bibliography

Bala, Suman, ed. *Women in the Novels of Shashi Deshpande.* New Delhi: Khosla, 2001.

Barche, G.D. "Indu: Another Sisyphus in *Roots and Shadows*," Dhawan, *Indian Women Novelists*.

Bhatt, Indira. "Shashi Deshpande's *The Dark Holds No Terrors*: A Study in Guilt Consciousness," Dhawan, *Indian Women Novelists*.

Desai, Anita. *Cry, the Peacock*. New Delhi: Orient Paperbacks, 1980.

Deshpande, Shashi. *Roots and Shadows.* Hyderabad: Orient Longman, 1983.

Dhar, T.N. "Portrait of a Marriage," Review of *That Long Silence. Indian Book Chronicle,* Jan.-Feb. 1990.

Dharkar, Rani. "Marriage as Purdah: Fictional Rendering of a Social Reality." *Margins of Erasure: Purdah in the Subcontinental Fiction in English*, ed. Jasbir Jain. New Delhi: Sterling, 1995.

Dhawan, R.K., ed. *Indian Women Novelists.* 3 Sets of 5, 6, 7 vols. respectively. New Delhi: Prestige, 1991-1995.

_____, ed. *The Fiction of Bharati Mukherjee: A Critical Symposium.* New Delhi: Prestige. 1996.

Dimri, Jaiwanti. "From Marriage to Murder: A Comparative Study of Bharati Mukherjee's *Wife* and *Jasmine*," Suman Bala, ed. *American Literature Today*. New Delhi: Prestige, 1994.

Inamdar, F.A. "Protagonists in Bharati Mukherjee's Novels, Dhawan, *Indian Women Novelists*, Set 1, Vol. I.

Kavya, B. "Marital Rape in Shashi Deshpande's Fiction," *Indian Streams Research Journal*, Vol. 2, Issue IV, 2012.

Mahida, Chintan. "Decoding Marital Problems in Anita Desai's Novels," *Quest International Multidisciplinary Research Journal*, 2.1 (2013): 154-60.

Mukherjee, Bharati. *Jasmine*. New Delhi: Penguin, 1990.

Patil, Ujwala. "The Theme of Marriage and Selfhood in *Roots and Shadows*," Dhawan. *Indian Women Novelists.* Set 1. Vol. 5.

Ramamoorti, P. "My Life is My Own: A Study of Shashi Deshpande's Women," Dhawan, *Indian Women Novelists*, Set 1, Vol. 5.

Sisodiya, Suraj Singh. "Theme of Marriage and Adjustment in Shashi Deshpande's Novels," *Journal of Literature, Culture and Media Studies*, Vol. II, Issue 4.

The Andar Mahal and the Zenana: A Study of R.N. Tagore's *The Home and the World* and Ismat Chughtai's "Lihaf"

SHUBNA CHAWLA
Res. Sch., Punjab University, Chandigarh

The concept of patriarchy and subjugation of women is a much discussed topic today and is central to many feminist theories. Though ideally women's position in a society is an indicator of its civilization and women should be taken as equal partners in the process of development, however for centuries women have been subjected to exploitation and subjugation, and have remained at the periphery. Literature is replete with terrible tales about exploitation, discrimination, inequality and violence inflicted upon women at all fronts.

Though in most cultures the restrictions on girls begin post-puberty, they become more stringent after marriage. The Victorian society is almost synonymous with the ideology of 'great men.' Women were allotted a subsidiary role, with patience and self-sacrifice the prime feminine virtues. Motherhood was idealised, alongside virginal innocence, but women were subject to pervasive denigration. In Indian society as well there are strong patriarchal traditions that persist in myriad hues, where life of women is constructed by ancient customs, where daughters are often regarded as a liability, and conditioned to believe that they are inferior and subordinate to men, whereas sons are idolised and celebrated. The daughter is supposed to remain in the custody and care of her parents, after marriage she becomes the property and responsibility of her husband.

Devoid of any property rights, economically dependent they are relegated to the confines of the house. The house itself is also the microcosm of the social constructions in the world outside. Within the household too they suffer oppression and suppression leading to the negation of their true self. Though the concept of patriarchy and a given defined space for women runs across countries and cultures, the women's problem however is not a homogeneous problem. There are nuances of class, religion, caste, race and sexual orientation which construct and define the lives of different women within contemporary cultures. Therefore the specificities of these require to be explored. The Paper attempts to problematise the feminist issues from a multicultural perspective by studying the 'Ander Mahal' in Rabindra Nath Tagore's novella, *The Home and the World* and the 'Zenana' in Ismat Chughtai's short story, "Lihaaf." The 'Andar Mahal' and the 'Zenana' represent the female inner space in a Hindu and a Muslim household respectively.

The Zenana, Andar mahal, purdah and seclusion of women within the house are a particular aspect of Indian family life. In much of northern and central India, Hindu and Muslim women followed and in rural India to a large extent still follow complex rules of veiling the body and avoidance of public appearance, especially in the presence of relatives linked by marriage and before strange men. There is a defined space within the house, exclusively demarcated for women often called the zenana or the andar mahal.

This 'gendering' of spaces is an important means by which social systems maintain the organization of Gender and it is inextricably linked to patterns of authority within the family. Though the specific form of purdah, zenana, etc. varies widely based on religion, region, class, and culture, and is supposedly connected with the idea of modesty for women, by minimizing the movement of women in public spaces and interaction of women with other males. So though ostensibly adopted to control female behaviour and sexuality it however invariably effectively also restricts her personal, social and economic activities both inside and outside her home.

By restricting women's mobility, purdah, zenana etc result not only in the social and physical isolation of women but they also have psychological and emotional ramifications. The lack of a strong social network places women in a position of vulnerability with their husband and their husband's family. These social and mobility restrictions also severely limit women's involvement in political decision-making as well.

According to some scholars Purdah was originally designed to protect women from being harassed and seen as sexual objects, to protect women's safety and honour while moving in public sphere and ensuring virtuous conduct. As Elizabeth White puts it, "purdah is an accommodation to and a means of perpetuating the perceived differences between the sexes: the male being self-reliant and aggressive, the female weak, irresponsible, and in need of protection." However Geraldine Brooks writes "in both cases [of spatial separation and veiling], women are expected to sacrifice their comfort and freedom, to service the requirements of male sexuality: either to repress or to stimulate the male sex urge."

Thus the significance of purdah and special segregation is not limited to family life; rather, these practices all involve restrictions on female activity and access to power and the control of vital resources in a male-dominated society. Restriction and restraint for women in virtually every aspect of life are the basic essentials of this segregation. In Indian society though both males and females are circumscribed in their actions by economic disabilities, hierarchical rules of deference in kinship groups, castes, and the larger society but for women who observe purdah, there are additional constraints which are both physical and psychological.

In this paper my attempt is to analyze the 'purdah,' the female inner space, not only physical but also psychological, in the 'Andar Mahal' in Rabindra Nath Tagore's novella *Ghare Baire* translated as *The Home and the World* and the 'Zenana' in Ismat Chughtai's short story "Lihaaf." The two writers, one male and the other female, coming from two different sociological and historical backgrounds, show how women from diverse cultures negotiate life within the 'Purdah.'

Tagore a male Bengali writer voices out women's issues and their condition in a patriarchal society through his works, 'Istrir patra,' 'Exercise Book,' *Chokher Bali*, *Ghare Baire* and others.

By giving voice to the women characters in his works, he is able to show that the needs and desires of a woman are no different from those of a man. He writes against the patriarchal set-up of the society, which not only restricts the physical movement of a woman inside the household, but also that which prevents a woman to transcend the boundaries of her married life, even psychologically.

Bimala, the female protagonist, in Tagore's *The Home and the World,* aspires to be a perfect traditional wife. She believes that service and devotion to one's husband are a woman's prime assets. She leads the life of an ideal Hindu wife for the first nine years of her married life. Her conditioning is such that she enjoys the 'golden cage' in which she says and asserts that "there was so much of space inside the cage for me that the whole world would not have been enough to contain it." It is only in retrospect, after having experienced the outside world, however, that she writes, "at least that's what I used to think then."

The backdrop of the novel is the Swadeshi movement in India and how the two male protagonists Nikhil and Sandip advocate Nationalism in their own way. Nikhil was of the belief that a country is independent only when every individual of the country is free. With firm faith in the premise he even wants, his wife, Bimala to move out of the 'purdah' and serve the world. Having internalized the gender constructions of the society, Bimala however conforms to the conventional Indian femininity.

Nikhil married Bimala despite the fact that she is from a poor family and has a dark complexion. Though Nikhil and

Bimala enjoy a peaceful marriage, Nikhil wants her to enter the outer world, believing their love would be true only if they recognize one another in the outer world. Bimala, conditioned to believe that purdah is her space in the house and that to be devoted to her husband is her sole duty, refuses to step out of the purdah. However, when Bimala attends a Swadeshi rally led by Sandip Babu, she insists he visit Nikhil's estate. Bimala and Sandip are attracted to one another, and Sandip decides to make his headquarters at the estate.

Bimala has all the material comforts as Begum Jan in 'Lihaf,' however in addition she also has a devoted husband who dotes on her and she is the Queen of the house. Nikhil buys her fancy slippers, would not have her touch his feet and also engages an English woman to teach her. Bimal feels no necessity of these things and actually has no regard for it, as she does not and cannot value them. Her tutoring as a woman has not prepared her to react or respond to such doting behaviour. She is conditioned to not even expect it rather to the contrary she feels that Nikhil is effeminate. This shows the extent of her conditioning that she couldn't think of him being a man enough because he is not aggressive, dotes on his wife and more so because he does not even visit the dancing girls.

Her repressed desire for a prince charming as her husband and the ingrained acceptance of a man as an aggressive partner in the relationship finds its fulfilment the moment she sets eyes on Sandip. She feels attracted to Sandip for his aggressive behaviour and passionate words. The golden cage suddenly becomes a prison and she strives to find ways out of it. As the story progresses, her heart which every woman is taught to negate comes to the fore. The Andar Mahal, however, does not give a woman the freedom which is available to men to fulfil such desires. Bimala however tries to fulfil her desires under the garb of Swadeshi. The physical movement out of the house was not prohibited to her but she herself never desired it. It is the desire for another male, the desire for Sandip, and not for Nikhil, that brings out the dormant woman in her. She was happy in her existence and consistently thwarted Nikhil's attempts to bring her out of the Andar Mahal. The stepping out of the threshold is not physical but mental, her negotiation of her feminine self happens vis-à-vis her relationship with Sandip. She goes beyond her conditioning, transgresses the boundaries of her Andar Mahal as she uses the pretext of the movement to meet Sandip and fulfils her repressed desires.

Lihaf too, deals with the unspeakable realities of the female space. It was written in 1941 by Ismat Chughtai. She displays a deep sympathy for the oppressed. Most of her works present radicalism and revolve around the exploitation of women and their economical and psychological problems.

In the story of a Muslim household, Begum Jan, the beautiful wife of a Nawab, though surrounded by all material comforts, fawning relatives and hordes of servants, nevertheless leads a lonely existence as her husband remains pre-occupied with fair-complexion, slender-waisted young boy students. She yearns for her husband's love and attention but getting none, withers and wilts away like a neglected plant till she finds solace in the arms of her maid-servant, Rabbu, and blossoms again. The Nawab was somewhat advanced in age and a very pious man. He was never known to indulge in decrepit habits like visiting prostitutes and had even performed Haj and helped others to perform it too. But for the Nawab, Begum Jan is nothing more than a piece of furniture installed in his house. She is left to pine away in loneliness while he has his rendezvous with the young boys he prefers to surround himself with. Thus all her dreams of spending a happy married life come to a naught; she is relegated to living her life on her canopied bed pining and yearning for her husband's love. She burns with envy as she watches the boys through the chinks of the drawing room doom. Like any conventional woman, she takes recourse to prayers and vows in order to reclaim her husband. She even tries practising her womanly charms but all her efforts are in vein. The woman limited by the defined space remained cold and lonely and her frustration grew day-by-day. She almost ceases to live till one day the maid-servant Rabbu pulls her from the brink of despair back to life again. Begum Jan's body began to fill and her beauty burst into bloom. Rabbu becomes Begum's constant companion forever, scratching her back, massaging her legs or head or various other body parts. By and by, even Rabbu's bed is placed in Begum Jan's room, next to the latter's bed-stead. So much is her dependence on Rabbu that when Rabbu visits her son, Begum Jan is distraught and dejected. Her body aches till the child narrator offers to scratch her back. Begum Jan presses the child tightly to herself, thus herself becoming an oppressor within the purdah in the process. Lihaf thus, courageously explores how a woman negotiates within the female inner space to survive in a patriarchal world.

The patriarchal world forms the identity of a person, on the basis of his or her behaviour and appearance. The behaviour and appearance are further constructions of this very world on the basis of the sex of the person, that is, male or female. The society is not concerned about the possibility of the Nawab being a homosexual till the time he performs all the rituals that the society expects him to. The young, neglected and physically unsatisfied Begum Jan, on the other hand, is forced to negotiate her sexual needs. Her 'itch' becomes a metaphor for her sexual desires and the only way through which Rabbu would touch her. The zenana then becomes her life in secret. She completely breaks away from the gender stereotype when a child is sent to the house to be looked after, she too is also exploited by Begum Jan. Begum Jan results in being an abusive parent within the zenana and hence destroying the image of zenana. That which was once thought of as a device to protect women from other men, is used by Chughtai to give Begum Jan autonomy over the household within the Zenana and liberate herself. Chughtai reveals the hypocrisy of the society. On one hand, it pushes a woman to compromise her sexuality and on the other hand, it talks of being something wrong with Begum Jan. However, the patriarchy seems to understand homosexuality and also provides space for it but it refuses to recognize it, and thus a homosexual relationship cannot exist (conscious ignorance). Though the oppressed becomes the oppressor in the story but this is how she negotiates and finds fulfilment within the zenana.

Women have generally been conditioned to be docile, sentimental, irrational, and dependent on men. They are taught to suppress their sexual energies and desires. Elaine Showalter in her *Mad Woman in The Attic*, associates the sexual energies of women with the menstrual cycle, which are considered by the patriarchal society as evil, and the woman is perceived as 'mad,' incarnation of the 'devil in the flesh.'

Both Tagore and Chughtai, belonging to two different worlds of region, religion and culture, and one a man the other a woman show how these energies lie dormant in a woman. Women however learn to negotiate within purdah to achieve some sense of gratification.

To conclude, the idea of desire is allowed to a male but not to a woman. In the case of Begum Jan, she cannot speak of her sexual exploits though similar to that of her husband's. In the case of Bimala the transgression is mental. Though apparently living a contented life, she suddenly sees the split in her personality, the two women inside her and also recognizes the one that dances to the tune of the snake charmer Sandip. Hence, both Begum Jan and Bimala belong to the upper class yet their existence is confined by patriarchy to the zenana. The female inner space is deprived of a fulfilling and a complete relationship. In both the cases the zenana and the andar mahal curb the woman's instincts and impulses. Thus, conforming to the social norms, both women are unable to explore their sexuality.

'What Their Place Should Be?' A Post-Feminist Reading of Deepti Naval's *The Silent Scream*

BHAGYASHREE S. VARMA
University of Mumbai

> For a long time I have hesitated to write a book on women. The subject is irritating, especially to women; and it is not new. Enough ink has been spilled in the quarreling over feminism, now practically over and perhaps we should say no more about it. It is still talked about however, for the voluminous nonsense uttered during the last century seems to have done little to illuminate the problem. After all, is there a problem? And if so, what is it? Are there women, really? Most assured the theory of the eternal feminine, still has its adherents who will whisper in your ear: "Even in Russia women still are women"; and other erudite persons—sometimes the very same—say if women still exist, if they will always exist, whether or not it is desirable that they should, what place they occupy in this world, what their place should be. (Beauvoir)

The feminist claim for a 'room of one's own' to relocate the 'mad woman in the attic' and liberate the singing caged birds from the prisons of patriarchy was adequately spread over the globe when an Indian actress, Deepti Naval, visited an asylum to observe the 'real' mentally disturbed women, to know 'madwoman' before rehearsing her own role of a madwoman for a film later on released as 'Ankahi.' She observed the woman in the madhouse and heard the saga of woman's untold (Ankahi) plight of survival. Deepti Naval's visit was interesting for two non-filmy reasons. The first was her sense of discovery—the discovery of a poet in the Platonic world of sanity. The second was a cathartic release of the collection of poems, *The Silent Scream*.

Deepti Naval had already published her first poetry collection in Hindi called *Lamha Lamha* which initiated her creative zeal into the literary world not as an actress but as a poet with John Keats' thirst for beauty. Her stay at the madhouse landed her into the thin border-region between the way sanity is defined and the way it is seen in women. Outside the walls of the asylum, a woman who raises a questioning glance at the invisible familial and social set up that systematically maddens women, throwing them into the unfathomable silence, Deepti published her anthology of poems in 2004 called *Black Wind and Other Poems*, with the inclusion of a very important section in it, *The Silent Scream*—twenty four fragments that unwrap the excluded forms of sanity.

Adrienne Rich brings out the essentialist positioning of woman in her argument for appropriating the politics of location, "Trying as women to see from the centre. A politics . . . of asking women's questions—we are not the woman question asked by someone else; we are the women who ask the questions." Rich further describes her memory of 'breaking down again and again the false male universal . . . (with the) anger, frustration . . . this disillusionment." (372-73)

Deepti Naval's disambiguation of 'the woman question,' as the questioning woman runs all through her visualized re-creations of woman's experience without and within the mad-house (not from the attic, thankfully), who seemed to look at herself introspectively asking 'to be or not to be is not the question but probably to 'become' or 'not to become' a woman is the question." In 'Goddess' the female voice begins her claim at the point of an epiphany,

> I am Kali! The Goddess! No one can conquer me!
> She pulled down the crown off the idol's head
> And wore it on herself,

> The crowds were aghast!
> They swore at her!
> Chased her with sticks, stones, screams
> But she slipped into the wilds
> Flying beyond their reach! (*Black Wind* 92)

The enlightening begins with not the epiphany but with the narrative of the seemingly blasphemous pose of woman who ventures to relish her merging with the wild in nature where she can hope to reign like a goddess and fearlessly moves on to escape the world she had outraged by crossing the threshold. The world is not that easily escapable and the 'maddening' crowd of

> villagers got her . . . caught her by the feet,
> Dragged her through the sludge . . .
> "She's too dangerous to be left free!"
> They signed on a piece of paper
> Dumped her in the loony bin!
> Wiped the vermillion off her forehead
> Chopped the long black hair
> Razed it to scalp
> Locked her behind the solid grill
> Left her squalling . . . on the cold dank floor. (*Black Wind* 93)

The confinement of woman was not only in the attic ages ago, even after she regained her paradise for a while, in the 'room of her own' her vulnerability did not vanish and the walls did not stop choking her breath and voice. Speaking of the African women's conditioning in his comment on 'The Damnation of Women' W.E.B. DuBois made a statement about women's victimization primarily emergent from the world's lack of acceptance of their freedom.

> The world wants healthy babies and intelligent workers. Today we refuse to allow the combination and force thousands of intelligent workers to go childless at a horrible expenditure of moral force, or we damn them if they break our idiotic conventions. Only at the sacrifice of intelligence and the chance to do their best work can

> the majority of modern women bear children. This is the damnation of women. All womanhood is hampered today because the world on which it is emerging is a world that tries to worship both virgins and mothers and in the end despises motherhood and despoils virgins . . . it wavers between the prostitute and the nun. Civilization must show two things: the glory and beauty of creating life and the need and duty of power and intelligence. (205)

Deepti believes women "perceive life little more intimately, as they are a little more sensitive, so if a woman writes openly about her desires . . . about her body and her perceptions, it will shock people. . . . How can you be open about it? How can you talk about it? You know, that's something so . . . mean, it just, I get exasperated. You know when I see attitudes like that. If a man talks about . . . I mean he can write books, and he can do all kinds of *Kama Sutra*, written by man; but if a woman writes about her sexuality, . . . she is judged, as a morally little you know, 'dheela' character, or not appropriate. Those are double standards. I see nothing wrong with the women if women writers who had guts to talk about, aspects of their lives, specially, when it comes to sexuality, with candor, and spontaneity and openness, I think it's perfectly fine." (Interview)

In 'Chasing a Scream' the woman's world is chased by the poet, haunted by 'a single scream' walking through the 'eerie length, corridor after corridor' to reach the

> Curled up bodies
> In rows of frayed blankets
> Behind locked doors . . . drugged in sleep
> . . . I pace through the dark, through fog, through fear
> Through stark verandahs splashed by light
> Sounds of my footsteps
> Echo . . . mindlessly I follow
> Bizarre patterns of light
> On the black and white tiles
> Till finally, at the end of night
> Trapped within the spotlight

The scream crashes into silence. (*Black Wind* 96)

I was sitting one day, after coming from a writer's meet, a literary festival and I was travelling with this lady and we were sent to the airport in the same car, waiting on the same table, for our different flights. And we talked normally throughout . . . as I was leaving, I said, "I am sorry, I didn't get, are you a film maker?" she said "No, I am a sex-worker." And I . . . and my flight was announced so I had to zip off, and I was like, you know, for a moment even I being an artist, being extremely broad-minded and having the complete conviction and mind and heart of an artist, even I was . . . a little, taken aback . . . by the way in which she said it. You know, because, she said it like I am an actress, I made movies, I write, I have written three books. She is a sex-worker . . . writing her autobiography. That's why she is here on this literary festival. And she has written that. But I was, it got me thinking that even I who claim to be an evolved independent woman writer, and an actress who had done some bold roles in my films, even I was a little taken aback. This is conditioning. This is our conditioning, but of course I admired her all the more, for saying it like with such normalness. I know there is some inescapable vulnerability because they are women writers. They get targeted more easily, for writing about their sexual experiences.

In a poem, you have to be frugal with words. A poem is also quite cathartic much more than a short story. Poetry is cathartic. Poetry churns you inside out several, several times, before you write it, when you are writing it, and even after you have written it. It keeps on churning you, because each time you revisit your written words, you are constantly revisiting the experience of having written that and then also you are constantly reanalyzing that experience which made you write that poem. And then constantly you feel like reworking on that poem. It doesn't really leave you. . . . Poetry is cathartic in many other ways.

A man tends to write about the world but when a woman writes we understand her world. Through woman we understand about her innermost world, and that covers the aspects of either domestic or . . . because women do tend to write personal. They are not afraid to write about their personal world. For men, except the personal they will be writing about everything else under the sun, but when it comes to personal they are hesitant. They do not sometimes have the guts to bear it all, whereas women do it with strength and women, it is true, are stronger in any case. (And she smiles with a pleasure, in her beautiful twinkling eyes). Women do have the strength to talk about their innermost feelings whether it's a sexuality, domesticity, their dreams and hopes, the shattering of their dreams, their traumas, because it takes a lot more guts to write about all that. You know it's easier to write about the geography of Bombay, the city houses, that many islands, how they started filling up the water, and then they made all this one piece of land, yes, I can go into research work and I can write many such things about the world, about things around me, but to say something personal it takes courage. And women I think are stronger beings emotionally. They do have this courage. The flow of Deepti's visualization smoothly moves in and out of the linguistic clarity and thematic complexity. "Personal stuff is lived stuff right? So there is more honesty there . . . they have to but there will be a time when there will be no male writers or female writers, there will be writers who write."

What the modern critics mean by "all art is representational" is a contextualized origin and creation of art . . . not only in the way something is politically representational, bringing you back to some social ethos, in which you are groomed as a writer, where you probably are suppressed, a constant politicization of your work as an artist or historically threatening your entity as a writer, something political in many cases,

Made of the Eastern sensibility and the Western influence as the very impressionable years of her college life were spent in the US, Deepti Naval was also impressed by Sylvia Plath, with her take on the confessional mode of writing as honestly poured personal stuff. Deepti's own voice as a writer involves contradictory dimensions since at once she is feminine but not so feminine in her writing, in the conservative sense of being feminine. Initially, in poetry she merges her feminine way of looking at love, man as the ultimate mirror to be loved, to live as beloved, and nature as the agency for conveying not only the sense of feminine world but evolving into the "disruptive force" and "shaking the symbolic" representational order as included in the discourse of feminine writing. Society, Religion, Culture or any systems that turned out to be a repressive pattern working to strangle the emerging expressions are all to be conquered only after the anguish and suffering through this 'creative' madness till the creativity in its peak, shapes it into a method. When asked about the way she conceived fragments of 'the Silent Scream' she frankly talks about the imagery and the memory mincing in the effect of the emotional trauma that she wanted to pen down with a certain sharpness to make her readers visualize more than analyze. She recalls the story of Mahasweta Devi that made a mark of courage, "the story of a woman who, confronting the set-up, says, Come, do the encounter. . . . I found it disturbing though." (Interview)

As an artist, painter poet and thinker Deepti does not have judgmental attitude towards the aberrations of life. She has that ability of mirroring what she finds around in the world, in multiple ways through her paintings, acting and poetry. What makes her more authentic is her stance without any 'ism.' She has no conscious articulation of nativism though she portrays Indian culture in her writings. She does not probe into the blindness of expressionism though she is aesthetically writing about the darker areas of mind, life and existence of women. She does not really incline towards the radical or even activist feminist stance though woman question occupies her concerns and prompts her to become a questioning woman. She is neither romantic nor anti-romantic though she smoothly slides into the rhetoric of beautifications in her narrative poetry and crosses equally softly the frames of emotive expressive exaltation of nature, human living and the blend of the two. Deepti is a product of her times, the child of East and West, the artist engaged in settling the woman whose place is between the two worlds of silence and screams, of gender and norms, of social and personal space. In the plain way, she is truly the world citizen. "I may not want to belong anywhere. I want to remain the individual voice that I am and this is the way I look at life. That is what I want to share with the world and I don't want to belong to any cult or any 'ism'!" (Interview) An infinite enthrallment in the historical arena of Art-Movies, Deepti the poet, the storyteller, walks on gracefully preserving her sanctuary of hope, quest and charisma, like a pigeon of love and peace.

Bibliography

Beauvoir, Simone De. *The Second Sex*, France, 1949.

DuBois, W.E.B. *The Essential Feminist Reader,* ed. Estelle B. Freedman, New York: Random House, 2007.

Naval, Deepti. *Black Wind and Other Poems*. MapinLit, 2004.

_____, *The Mad Tibetan: Stories From Then And Now*, Amaryllis, 2011.

_____. Interview, *Muse India,* Nov-Dec. 2015

Rich, Adrienne. "Notes towards a Politics of Location," *The Essential Feminist Reader*, ed. Estelle B. Freedman, New York: Random House, 2007.

The Indian Diaspora: A Pacific Perspective*

SATENDRA NANDAN
ANU, Canberra, Australia

More than a decade ago I was invited to Delhi to participate and celebrate the Inaugural Pravasi Bharatiya Divas on 9 January 2003. It was a magnificent and momentous occasion; around 2000 overseas Indians from 63 countries, continents and islands, were present, each remembering and paying tribute to Mother India from which their ancestors or they had migrated to many parts of the world. Hardly any modern nation doesn't have a person of Indian descent in its society, not to mention the Red Indians or Ameri-Indians.

Mr. Atal Bihari Vajpayee was the Prime Minister of India and he stood tall among his colourful comrades. I still remember the two poetic lines he flourished:

Hum sab hain ek pariwar;
Khula hamesha hamara dwar!

It was truly a celebratory and generous occasion and there was quite a contingent from the Pacific, mainly Fiji and New Zealand, including the future Governor-General of New Zealand, Dr Anand Satyanand.

This is my second Pravasi Bharatiya Divas—perhaps a prelude to the annual occasion in January in Delhi. I'm happy to be here amongst you all and delighted that this is being held in Sydney, a Pacific city with the Harbour Bridge as its bridging symbol: on which we can hang our coats of the past and stitch a world for the future.

On that first occasion, I remember listening to Amartya Sen and V.S. Naipaul, the two recent Nobel laureates of Indian origin, representing two phases of the Indian Diaspora—Naipaul's sensibility has its roots in the Indenture experience, 1830-1920; Sen is the product of the post-Independence India, the modern diaspora, now belatedly part of Australia.

But there's an Ancient Indian Diaspora which is relevant to our inheritance in this part of the world. It's almost two millennia old—that is how we've Bali and Borubodur—pilgrims and teachers who travelled to spread the noble philosophy of the spiritual awakenings of India and spread the word long before the more recent religions began creating a converted world. They structured societies, shaped kingdoms and cultivated civilizations.

And even before that our terrestrial connections with the original people of Australia when the island continent was an integral part of the vast Asian landmass. Geography more than history then determined the configurations of world consciousness: The idea of 'discovery' is deeply suspect. There were worlds and civilizations on the move long before Europe 'discovered' that the world was round and the earth revolved round the sun.

But today in our contemporary and cosmopolitan world, I wish to talk briefly about the Indenture Diaspora: from the 1830s this system was introduced to transport around 2 million Indians to many parts of the British, Dutch and French colonies. From 1879-1920 over 60,000 children, women and men, were transplanted in the islands of Fiji to serve the British and Australian interests in economic and political terms and to protect the way of life of the indigenous community.

This is a unique fragment in imperial history known for genocide and decimation of native populations so painfully explored and apologized for today. To have uprooted communities 10,000 miles away from a sub-continent to bring them across the seven seas, to prevent the dislocation of native population on the small islands of the South Pacific: Is there another story of such a migration in history?

Most of these Indians were illiterate; they had little idea of history, less of geography; they had never seen a ship, a sea-wave or an island. Fiji is a revealing case—the pre-colonial, the colonial and the postcolonial co-exist even today. Ninety percent of all land in Fiji is communally owned, exactly the opposite in Australia where terra nullius ruled unchallenged at least into the 1990s. This deepest dispossession of the first Fijians did not take place in Fiji—a page of history to be proud of. Yet, all the racist coups in Fiji were shamelessly perpetrated by indigenous elite whose greed for power and privilege exceeded their ideas of freedom and development—the sacrifices, accommodation a modern nation makes to enjoy and ensure the freedoms of all its citizens.

Fiji's first governor Sir Arthur Gordon created a 'Gordonian' knot and introduced the policy of protecting native interests, especially land, from his rapacious compatriots once Fiji became a crown colony; indeed in 1874 Fiji was ceded to Queen Victoria—perhaps the only case in colonial history when a Deed of Cession of sovereignty is celebrated with special ties to the British Crown. Gordon had an experience of indentured Indians in the islands of Mauritius and Trinidad: how a barren colony could become prosperous through the labour of a displaced people cruelly called 'coolies.' You can hear the term even today in India used without any sensitivity or shame to its historical irony. Yet the Father of India was most prophetically called the coolie barrister!

Thereby of course hang many a tale until the first Fijian coups by a third-ranking colonel of the Royal Fiji Military Forces. For instance, no-one cared for the dislocation of the indentured Indians who had lived in their villages for millennia, barely travelling beyond five kilometres of their ancient boundaries. Yet they were flung all over the empire with little consideration for their fate or future. These were men and women in their prime of life. 'Stolen generations' have echoes beyond our island continent.

Indenture was one step away from slavery—it had an expiry date: after ten years of agreement, you may get a passage back to India. No-one of Indian origin has, in my readings, written a comprehensive human history of these one hundred years of servitude. The word 'girmit' comes from the pidgin distortion of the word 'agreement,' sealed with the leftthumbmark.

Gandhi, whose day of return to India on January 9, after 21 years among the girmityas and small merchants in South Africa is now commemorated as the Pravasi Bharatiya Divas. It is a deeply significant memorial to the greatest and noblest Indian. To think he came from the business caste and was a lawyer boggles the mind and baulks the imagination in the context of today's many business operators and professionals—NSW is not a bad place to begin. His most formative years were spent among the indentured and small merchants in a racially discriminated and divided country. To understand this is to realize the achievement of the First Girmitya, 'pahila girmitya,' as he's sometimes called; and is the Father of modern India.

How deeply he civilized imperial powers and empowered the dispossessed and marginalized peoples worldwide. It is a narrative of epic grandeur. It is a girmit legacy too. He never said that the Emperor had no clothes; instead he remarked half-nakedly, with an extraordinary power of observation, that the Emperor is wearing enough clothes for both of us! He's the pilgrim hero of this diaspora beyond the Indian ocean: one with a lathi, not with bows and arrows or the deadly mace of Brigadier-General Hanuman.

In the October 25 issue of the weekly *Guardian* an article says how 'Gandhi's blanking of the Africans is the black hole at the heart of his saintly mythology.' The writer, aptly named Patrick French, misses the point. The point is precisely that of the human soul which doesn't belong to any race or nation. The soul-force of a single person can achieve miracles—it's limitless with infinite possibilities but no boundaries—the *atman* is an atom containing unfathomable energy, both creative and destructive. It has no borders or barriers. Gandhi gave a war-weary, colonially corrupt and corrupting world, a way out. He tried it with a people he knew best but he also knew his example will inspire humanity for generations yet unborn, black and white, brown and yellow, on every continent and on many an island.

So what is unique yet universal that the Indian Diaspora can contribute to this part of our global existence? This was a question I'd raised in my talk in Delhi a decade ago. I feel they have a deeper resonance and relevance to Australasia. Indian mind, as we all know, had been severely colonized over centuries—colonialism like the bee sucked the nectar to make honey but it also pollinated the flower and left its sting in not a few decaying monoliths among its ambitious and scattered ruins.

When I first went to Delhi, more than fifty years ago, I was astonished to see students reading only English literature in their Honours classes at the capital university, 12 years after Independence and Partition. One of the greatest struggles for freedom and the brutal imperial crime of Partition had disappeared in the dust storms of Delhi and the stained dawn of Indian renaissance.

Today all that has changed quite radically and Indian writers, artists, activists, academics, scientists, professionals, public servants, business men and women have made a vital difference. The global language English has been a more creative weapon than missiles in shaping our thinking and imagining. And through English a new awareness of India is growing in the mind of Australasia. The population has quadrupled and the weariness of the Independence struggle is replaced by a nation's nascent and latent energy of deeper critical self-awareness.

Trade and business are important; professions are significant; military and strategic alliances can be meaningful. But these arrangements can change overnight. Japan is a case in point: in 1905 it is the first Asian nation to defeat a European power, Russia; within 40 years in 1945, it became an abject and defeated colony of another imperialism, American, due to its hubris and imitation of the imprints of imperialism.

So is there something different that the Indian diaspora can contribute—different from European, American, Chinese, Japanese worldviews—as India did in its ancient diaspora? That religious view of the world is no longer adequate—the delights and discontents of democracy and joys of secularism are now part of our daily bread. The universe is enlarging; so is our knowledge of the stem-cell and the cosmos.

India, to a large extent, did it without, I feel, sacrificing its sacred soul—a soul made of many streams and myriad dreams. Bollywood is generally a superficial but popular expression of this dynamic cultural palimpsest of civilizations. Think for a moment: Ancient Europe was converted to Christianity, Arabia to Islam, China to Communism but in India very distinct and different sources of the self have been developing for millennia, with all its detritus of caste and customs, religious humbug and cosmic kidding, but the quintessence of India remains. Its many vulnerabilities strengthen its inner resources: nothing much grows on marbled floors.

Most Indians always thought of going to England, then Europe, then America, followed by Canada. This is where the diasporan now is. Australasia is a late discovery for reasons of colour and imaginative courage. Think different, Gandhi showed. Discover a new world by sailing in a new direction.

If Indians studied their history well, they would have come to this island continent long ago—they came to the Indonesian islands but because they thought the world was flat, taking their ships further south could make them disappear without a trace in an oceanic chasm. So they never explored it further—if they had we could have a better Aussie cricket team here today!

But be that as it may, I wish to talk a bit about the two talks I heard at that first Pravasi Bharatiya Divas in Delhi in January 2003. Amratya Sen talked about the kupamanduka, frogs in a well—a warning against isolationism that recurs in several old Sanskrit texts, told Sen. He was referring to an attitude in a segment of Indian intelligentsia which has a very constricted view of Indian heritage and history. He argued that the scientific, cultural, political, economic, rationalistic and civil history of the world would have been very limited indeed had we lived like well-frogs.

The celebration of Indian civilization can and must go hand in hand with an affirmation of India's active role in a global world. The existence of a large diaspora abroad is itself a part of India's interactive presence. In short we cannot allow ourselves to be diminished by any ideology that limits our shared and unfinished humanity. This view of India has done enormous damage to the Indian image and it's not the sign of a confident and creative nation and Indians everywhere pay a psychological price when ugly publicity is spread across our internetted world with which we're inexorably interconnected. 2000 people killed in the state of Gujarat in 2002 had cast a dark shadow on that first Pravasi Bharatiya Divas in New Delhi in 2003.

I vividly recall Sen using that metaphor, frogs in a well, to describe aspects of a fundamentalist sensibility. It is both moronic and an oxymoron. Sen was for a secular democracy giving security and prosperity to its citizens and liberty to the individuals struggling for human rights that cuts across all national borders like our climatic concerns or human rights.

It is in this that Indian Diaspora can make signal and singular contribution to our growing Australian civilization—from the ancient Aboriginal roots to the green shoots of migrants. And yet issues of Aboriginal situation, Fijian coups and asylum seekers hardly feature in our Diaspora discussions. I wonder why no Aboriginal leader or thinker is part of this diaspora in Sydney? Or a

Pacific statesman? Surely Indian diaspora in Australasia must include the South Pacific leaders as part of our conversation.

We make excellent public servants, babus, and shopkeepers but challenging the status quo is not our concern as long as we've some status, others can have the quo. So I think we in the diaspora could afford a few public intellectuals in Australasia. Anyone who has read even a few essays in Sen's *The Argumentative Indian* would discover a rich and remarkable tradition of the rational and scientific Indian mind's contributions to the world culture.

Too much of mawkish religiosity has created a veil that hides the great and secular vision of our universe and the Indians were pioneers—there. The guru-syndrome has often been gross and gratuitously galling and self-deceiving. It makes India small: the wonder of the world, so resplendently evoked in the lines of the Vedas, is lost in false values of exclusive cultural identity. A sure sign of a people lacking in confidence in their acts of creativity and imagination and the daring of their ancestors.

And this brings me to Vidia Naipual—the first person of Indian origin to win a Nobel prize in Literature after Tagore exactly a hundred years ago in 1913. Not that this is the ultimate accolade—after all, Gandhi never got the Nobel for Peace but Kissinger did! But that says more about the Prize committee not the individual—and Gandhi's quip that 'western civilization will be good idea' is still valid.

Naipaul, coming from the Indenture diaspora, is one of the sharpest critics of India and its diaspora. His talk in Delhi, I recall, was on Ananda Coomaraswamy, whose work is hardly remembered and studied in India. His complaint was that even the Banaras Hindu University, where Coomaraswamy taught, couldn't keep his papers in its archives for future scholars. He was the author of *The Dance of Shiva*, a seminal text on Indian thought and culture.

To Naipaul this was a great loss—not of El Dorado but of Indian scholarship. And it is this he laments deeply. Is the country too full of ruins, mainly of temples and tombs? We all know the great universities of the world were created from churches and monasteries; why did Indian civilization fail to build universities and institutions of democracy—huge palaces, forts, tombs, temples everywhere but no great institutions of science and art, writing and research, of serious inquiries and scholarship, in the markings of civilizations where civil liberties should be paramount and scientific inquiry is given its due.

Naipaul mistakenly took Gandhi to task for leaving nothing of enduring value in South Africa. Yet, Gandhi's was one life that made him weep. But Gandhi was made in the imperial world, and even he had his limitations.

Today of course Indian writers, scholars, artists, scientists, political thinkers are shaping the contours of thoughts, and ideas of modernity. It's here, I think, the Indian Diaspora can make lasting contributions to Australasian educational landscapes, intellectual horizons and international relations.

*

The flowering of the Indian democracy is the greatest story of our world—no country faced greater challenges after its brutal and unnecessary vivisection, but today, with all its problems, a multitudinous, multilayered political culture has emerged against the tragedies of partition, caste, patriarchy, Cold War, etc. India remains an example in our increasingly plural, multifaceted, multiplex global search for a fairer and better world.

Fiji is a small island nation in the vast Pacific Ocean. Its new constitution gives one hope that Fiji can move towards a democratic future after four coups—three of them unnecessary and racist—against the girmit people and their defenceless dependents. It seems to me the Australasian Indian diaspora and India can play a positive role in making Fiji a truly multicultural society of promise and achievements unheard of in the South Pacific.

The diaspora can contribute in every field of endeavour and human relationships without the crutches of race and religion, caste or colour.

The Fijian diaspora is another story for another occasion. One hopes this occasion will arouse deeper interest in Fiji and the Indian roots and routes of the diaspora will be written, read and contemplated on with some serious understanding: For there's no country, big or small, like Fiji in Australasia .

We can, with others, give the Pacific its true meaning—generosity of heart and the peace of mind. And begin to understand the new horizons before us. This is a great gift of all our ancestors.

**Professor Satendra Nandan was invited to the Regional Overseas Indian conference organized in Sydney, November 10-12, 2013, to give a talk. Satendra is a former member of Parliament and cabinet minister of Fiji; he was also a commissioner to help draft a new constitution of Fiji in 2012. Currently he's a Professor Emeritus at the Donald Horne Institute for creative research and culture, Faculty of Arts and Design, University of Canberra, and an Adjunct Professor, Centre for Applied Philosophy and Professional Ethics, CSU and Melbourne.*

Indo-Fijian Diaspora: Labour Migration from Indian Continent

SRIDHAR MADDI
Research Scholar, Kakatiya University, Warangal
BITLA SRINIVASULU
B.V. Raju Institute of Technology, Narsapur

"Diaspora" has been drawn from Greek meaning of dispersal and signifies a voluntary or forcible movement of the people from the native land into new regions. It represents to "anybody living outside their native land." Under Colonialism, "Diaspora" has become à very varied movement involving a temporary or permanent movement of Europeans all over the world which has led to colonial settlement. By the effect the ensuing economic exploitation of the settled areas emerged a large amount of labour that could not be fulfilled by the local population. This has resulted in the enslavement of colonial people and their relocation to places in the British colonies. After slavery is abolished, the continued demand for workers has created contractual labour. This has produced large bodies of people from the poorer areas of India, China and others to move to West Indies, Eastern and Southern Africa, Malaya, Fiji etc.

Today, with the advancements of technology, traveling has become easier and faster. Distances are no more of concern. Simultaneously the meaning of diaspora too underwent change and lost its original connotation. William Safran's definition is much more comprehensive and provides context to the development of ideas on the diaspora. Safran suggests that the concept of diaspora can be applied to expatriate communities whose members share several of the following characteristics:

1. They or their ancestors have dispersed from a specific original "Centre" to two or more foreign regions.
2. They retain a collective memory, vision or myth about their original homeland.
3. They believe they are not and perhaps cannot be fully accepted by their host society and therefore feel partly alienated and insulated from it.
4. They regard their ancestral homeland as their true, ideal home and a place to which they or their descendants would eventually return when conditions are appropriate.
5. They believe that they should be committed to homeland and its safety and prosperity.
6. They continue to relate personally or vicariously, to that homeland in one way or another, and their ethno communal consciousness and solidarity are importantly defined by the existence of such a relationship (Nelson).

Robin Cohen classifies Diaspora into Victim Diasporas, Labour Diasporas, Imperial Diasporas, Trade Diasporas, Homeland Diasporas and Cultural Diasporas. The categories of Diaspora reflect the particular cause of migration, associated with particular groups of people. So for example, the Africans through their experience of slavery have been noted to be victims of extremely aggressive transmigration policies. Cohen finds a common element in all forms of Diaspora; these are people who live outside their "natal (or imagined natal) territories" and their traditional homelands are reflected deeply in the languages they speak, religion they adopt, and cultures they produce.

Indian Diaspora can be classified into two kinds: Forced Migration to Africa, Fiji or the Caribbean as indentured labour in the 18th and 19th centuries; and Voluntary Migration to U.S.A., U.K., Canada or other European countries for professional or academic purposes. According to Amitav Ghosh, "the Indian Diaspora is one of the most important demographic dislocations of Modern Times." The forced migration Diaspora consisted of underprivileged and subaltern classes with a one-way ticket to a distant diasporic settlement. In those days, return to Native land is next to impossible due to lack of proper means of transportation, economic deficiency, and vast distances. So the physical distance has become a psychological alienation, and the homeland has become the sacred icon in the diasporic imagination of the authors.

But Voluntary Migration Diaspora was the result of man's choice and inclination towards material gains, professional and business interests. It is particularly a representation of the privileged with access to contemporary advanced technology and communication. Here, no dearth of money or means is visible. Rather economic and lifestyle advantages are facilitated by the multiple visas and frequent flyer utilities.

It is clear that the notion of diaspora is used to refer a wide range of historical and contemporary phenomena. Diaspora exists and is reproduced in everything that creates a bond in a place, among those who want to group together and maintain from a distance, relations with other groups installed in other places, but having the same identity. This bond can come in different forms, such as family, community, religious bonds or shared memory of a catastrophe or trauma suffered by members of the diaspora or the forebears. A diaspora has a symbolic and iconographic capital that enables it to reproduce and overcome the obstacle of distance separating its communities. Diaspora areas and territories must be gauged first in the host country, where the community bond plays the essential role, then in the country or territory of origin—a pole of attraction—through memory. Thus the term diaspora plays more of a metaphorical than an instrumental role.

In India the sacred Hindu scriptures prohibited crossing the seas. Thus there is no large-scale emigration until the 19th century. However, Indian emigration during the 19th and early 20th centuries is unprecedented. It is the European imperialist expansion that has created condition for emigration in large numbers. Due to this, India witnessed massive movements of people from India to other parts of the world. Indentured labour, a distinct pattern of emigration is identifiable during the colonial period.

The diaspora is a performance of the narrative acts of inscribing place, people, event, incident, accident, coincidence, causality and the official record in contradictory practices of living/dying, dislocation as a cycle. History has become the originator narrative for the diaspora as well as of the actual movement and then it engages in the task of recording, interpreting and reading the process over and over again. For example, in the colonizing of India and cession of Fiji to Britain, the British Empire forms the nexus between two colonies and is empowered by imperialism to provide Indian indentured labour and later free immigrants from India to Fiji. Questions of labour, capital and land and their various interpolations in India, Fiji and in Britain, began the process of a diasporic removal of people through official documentation to engage in the practices of Indenture. A diaspora begins with a moment of displacement with its insistent reasons for causality that begins the remove of a people from a place.

Colonialism institutionalized negative practices in Fiji between Indo-Fijians and indigenous Fijians. This has taken many forms and can be traced to the institution of "divide and rule" of British colonial practice throughout its empire. Brij Lal outlines the "divide and rule" practice in terms of the fact that "Government policy has done nothing to encourage the two groups to cross each other's boundary. The gulf between the two communities that has resulted from culture, language, and religion were exacerbated by government policy, which made no attempt to draw them together into truly common bonds of citizenship" (107).

Teresia Teaiwa cites abdication of personal responsibility among Indo-Fijians and Fijians to learn about culture, language and enter into social discourse with the other. She quotes Indo-Fijian poet and academic Sudesh Mishra on his admission that in high school a choice to learn Fijian has been thwarted as between, 'teacher and pupil, there was an abdication of responsibility from both sides.' (Teaiwa 98) Paul Geraghty points out the imbalance in acquiring language skills and acknowledging knowledge of the 'other' being tilted against Fijians. However, various other writers (e.g. Roth 40; Quain 8; Mayer 180: Moag 130) have commented on the common knowledge of Fijian among Fiji Indians. Even in the cane-growing areas, where knowledge of Hindi amongst Fijians is highest, knowledge of Fijian by Indians is still greater' (Geraghty 7). The coups of 1987 and 2000 brought with them a mass exodus and diasporic dislocation that is important in the study of the second shift diaspora from Fiji to places like Liverpool in Sydney, Australia.

In the Indo-Fijian diaspora there have been removals and shifts based on issues such as land, migrations, rise and fall of crops like sugar, timber, banana and copra. Historical/political upheavals and conditions in the 1970s have linked to general elections and Fijian nationalism between 1974 and 1977 and thereafter, the 1987/2000 coups and the 1990 Constitution, have engendered or added to these shifts and removals. There is now significant internal migration of the Indo-Fijian diaspora as part of the re-location of mostly farming groups due to non-renewal of leases on their land. The post-1987 indigenous fundamentalism institutionalized by the 1990 Constitution was another decisive factor in determining migration trends, both to the second shift locations or to new locations within Fiji. The promulgation of a fairer Constitution in 1997 is seen as being equally decisive in dictating the trends in Indo-Fijian migration from Fiji until the political upheavals and civil unrest of 2000.

In the historical siting of Indo-Fijian diaspora, it is important to begin with a document of their first dislocation. The success of an indentured workforce in the West Indies has been taken as an example by Sir Arthur Gordon, Fiji's first Governor, for an easy and workable system to solve Fiji's labour shortage. In a speech to planters at a meeting organized to gain their consent for Indian indentured labourers on September 8 1878, Gordon began on the following premise: 'An ample and steady supply of labour is absolutely essential to the Colony. From when and under what management shall we obtain it most certainly, most cheaply and with the least probability of abuse?' (Girmit Council 6)

This sub-section provides an overview of Indo-Fijian diaspora's cultural and educational history. Brij Lal provides a succinct historical background of the prevailing literary culture and the educational history of the Indo-Fijian diaspora. The starting point according to Lal is that 'Indians had already started to reconstitute fragments of their ancestral culture and fashion a new moral universe, helped after the turn of the 19th century by visiting religious figures from India.' (Lal 57)

With the loss of their home and absence of homeland, these Indians have depended on the Gita, the *Ramayana*, the Hanuman Chalisa and the Mahabharata as Satendra Nandan explains: 'We have lived by such stories, our ancient epics—first our grandparents, then our mothers and fathers, now our political leaders. Our fate in Fiji had echoes of the Ramayana: exile, suffering, separation, battles but no return.' Very often they compared their exilic life with that of Ram's banishment from Ayodhya and thereby gave their act as something sacred and heroic.

Brij Lal prefaces the growth of a literary culture with the importance of religion in maintaining overseas Indian cultural identity, so that 'In Fiji by the 1890s, most Indian settlements had the basic texts of popular Hinduism' (55). Of these popular texts the 'most significant of all [was], Tulsidas' *Ramcharitramanas,* the story of Lord Rama in some 10,000 lines of verse in the Avadhi dialect of Hindi familiar to most of the North Indian migrants' (56). Brij Lal goes on to add:

> Rama's story struck a particular chord with the Fiji Indians. Rama was exiled for fourteen years for no fault of his own, but he did return; good ultimately did triumph over evil. His story gave them hope and consolation: one day, their ordeal, too, would come to an end. (55-56)

Lal places this early affinity with Rama's banishment within the context of other texts in the early period of indenture until the 1920s when systematic religious, cultural and educational organizations formed and began their roles as providers and controllers of education, literature and other art forms. The origins of education based in Indian/Muslim religious/cultural traditions according to Lal was due to 'colonial indifference' and the fact that the 'Indian's marked lack of enthusiasm for Christian schools in the early years, helped produce a distinctively 'Indian' education for the children.' (57) The two main Hindu organizations, the Sanatan Dharma and Arya Samaj 'were joined in 1920 by Muslim, South Indian, Guajarati and Sikh organizations' (56). As a beginning this is an important marker of Indo-Fijian identity that writes, and speaks to this common cultural past in education and by extension in literature.

Indians have moved to every corner of the world including Fiji; wherever they have moved, left a mark of India and its culture among people of other lands and homelands. Labourers who have migrated from India to Fiji are adapted to Indo-Fijian culture and education. Colonial era encouraged many Fijians against each other. It has also created differences among Indians and Fijians.

Bibliography

Ahmad, Aizaz. *In Theory: Classes Nations, Literatures*, O.U.P., 1992.

Ashcroft, Bill, Pal Ahluwalia, Edward Said, *The Paradox of Identity*, Routledge, London & New York 1999, 31-56.

Bhabha, Homi, *The Location of Culture*, London, 1994.

Dentseh, Andse. *An Area of Darkness*. London, 1964, 31.

Ghosh, Amitav, *The Hungry Tide*, Delhi: Ravi Dayal Pub. 2004.

_____. *The Ghost of Mrs. Gandhi in the Imam and the Indian*. Ravi Dayal, New Delhi, 2002, 51.

_____. 'The Diaspora in Indian Culture,' *The Imam and the Indian*, Ravi Dayal and Permanent Black, Delhi: 2002, 243.

Hall, Stuart. 'Cultural Identity and Diaspora in Patrick White and Laura Christmas, ed., Colonial Discourses and Post-Colonial Theory: A Reader, New York: Columbia University Press, 1994), 401.

Mehta, Suketu, *Maximum City*, Viking, Penguin, 2004, 13.

Naipaul, V.S. *A House for Mr. Biswas*. Penguin, 1969, 14.

Raza, Rahi Masoom. *Sheeshe Ke Makan Vale*, ed. Kunvar Pal Singh, Delhi: Vani Pub., 2001.

Robin, Cohen. *Global Diasporas: An Introduction*. London: UCL Press, 1997.

Rushdie, Salman. *Shame*. Picader, Rupa, 1983, 283.

William, Safran cited Satendra Nandan: 'Diasporic Consciousness,' *Interrogative Post-Colonial Column Theory, Text and Context*, ed. Harish Trivedi and Meenakshi Mukherjee, Indian Institute of Advanced Studies 1996), 53.

Reflection of Diaspora in Postcolonial Approaches: A Conceptual Study

NITESH NARNOLIA & MOUSAM
Res. Sch., Central University of Gujarat, Gandhinagar

Postcolonial is a broad term. It is a study of the effects of colonialism on cultures and societies. It is concerned with both how European nations conquered and controlled 'Third World' nations and how these nations responded and resisted these European powers. Post-colonialism, as a theory and as a study of political and cultural change has gone through a continuous change through three stages:

1) An initial awareness of the social, psychological and cultural inferiority enforced by being in a colonized state;
2) The struggle of ethnic, cultural and political autonomy and
3) A growing awareness of cultural overlapped and hybridity.

The term 'postcolonial' is defined differently by many critics. Many critics define 'post-colonial' as a social condition or a temporal period; while others define 'postcolonial' as a political critique of modernity and colonialism that can be understood through the analysis of the links between power and knowledge.

Postcolonialism as a social condition provides an understanding of the histories of migration and displacement since the time of colonialism and independence. On the other hand, postcolonial as a political critique attempts to define and to deconstruct the Eurocentric discourses of colonialism, nationalism and modernity through challenging the western narratives of history and re-establishing the relationship between power and knowledge. In this process of deconstruction, postcolonial studies seems to distract from the binary study of colonial and anti-colonial that establishes 'elite nationalism' that do not deconstruct the Eurocentric logic of knowledge that continuous to rule anti-colonial politics. Therefore, postcolonial studies, as a field of study of subaltern studies, is distinguished by its focus on nation and modernity.

Subaltern studies scholars try to demolish the hegemony of the bourgeois class in the constructing the postcolonial nation. Postcolonial feminist studies scholars, such as Partha Chatterjee and Gayatri Spivak, also supported the approach of subaltern studies scholars and argued that "nationalism is derivative and complicit with colonialism and consequently that anticolonial bourgeois nationalism has failed to represent subaltern subject within the nation" (Desai 10).

In contrast to these non-elite subjects of subaltern studies, diasporic study of Postcolonialism argued in favour of Eurocentric approaches to nationalism. Diaspora is a process of the voluntary or enforced migration of people from their native homeland. The postcolonial diasporic migrants often have been the members of the bourgeoisie who have remained invested in employing this Eurocentric construction of cultural difference.

During British colonialism, South Asians migrated to Britain and other parts of the commonwealth, including Africa, Canada and Caribbean. After independence and the end of the colonialism, more professional-class of South-Asian migrated to the West and their educational training made them attractive for Western economies. This bourgeois class has developed transnational space in the last half of the century and formed a specific history of colonialism. According to Partha Chatterjee, it is this class that became the Indian National bourgeoisie that has transnational connections after several generations.

With independence, this class gained access to education but did not get any promise of employment and access to modernity. The postcolonial economy did not support the aspirations of this under-employed class that decided to migrate in order to fulfil its desires and to realize its potentials. This English speaking middle class was first formulated by colonialism and then reformulated by anti-colonial nationalism which indulged them in trans-nationality in postcolonial migration.

Several postcolonial scholars, such as Homi Bhabha, have tried to understand the relationship between postcoloniality and transnational migration. Postcolonial Diasporas mark the return of the repressed in Bhabha's works. The migration of Asian to Britain, results directly from aftermath of colonialism in Britain where they were denied citizenship and are excluded from the nation because of the history of colonialism.

In postcolonial studies Diaspora is used in lower case. The authors use the term "diaspora" for the process of western or European colonization. Diaspora is "the voluntary or forcible movement of people from their homelands into new regions." Under colonialism, diaspora is a multifarious movement, which involves:

- The temporary or permanent movement of Europeans all over the world, leading to colonial settlements. Consequently, the economic exploitation of the settled areas demanded large amounts of labour that could not be fulfilled by the local people. That led to:
- The diaspora resulting from the enslavement of African and their relocation to place like the British colonies. After slavery was outlawed, the continued demand for workers created indentured labour, which produced:
- Large bodies from poor areas of India, China to the West Indies, Malaya, Fiji, Eastern and Southern Africa and South East Asia etc.

Further, the authors note that diaspora is of importance to postcolonial studies because the descendants of these people produced unique cultures which are maintained and built on the perceptions of their original cultures.

Postcolonial scholars and critics are still struggling to develop an appropriate term for the socio-cultural dislocations as a result of colonialism and nation-building process, dislocations which are inherited in the history of indenture and slavery, and the expulsion of indigenous people from their ancestral lands. Of course, in addressing these dislocations, postcolonial critics do not deal with victimization or victims; rather they pay attention to how historically displaced people have developed their inventive tactics for transforming the experiences of dislocation into vibrant and revolutionary forms of political and cultural life.

Thus, in the last fifteen years, diaspora had emerged as a highly appreciated term among postcolonial scholars. Scholars such as Paul Gilroy, Floya Anthias, Stuart Hall, Carole Boyce Davies, Rey Chow, Smaro Kamboureli, Diana Brydon and Rinaldo Walcott all seem to be sharing their hopes that diaspora studies will help in foregrounding the cultural practices of both forcefully exiled and voluntarily migrant people, that diaspora studies will help in challenging certain assumptions about ethnicity, race, and national boundaries, and also that diaspora studies will help in forging new links between emergent critical methodologies and contemporary movements. The postcolonial diaspora might be best understood not as self-evident socio-cultural phenomenon, but as figures which may help us to better read the politics of specific racialized collectivities within the modern West.

One way of introducing the postcolonial diaspora is to accept the fact that postcolonial reading is a body of debate which never exhibits an original investment in the nation-state as the mater trope of resistance. This claim might find complicated backing from different texts as *The Wretched of the Earth, Imagined Communities* and *The Empire Writes Back.* The appearance of the postcolonial diaspora would be a mark of new disenchantment with nation-based articulations of postcolonialism, a disenchantment which we might describe through three factors:

1. The first factor is a renewed awareness, which was born of the vital inventions of Feminist, Marxist, and queer Postcolonialism and of the patriarchal, classicist, ethnocentric and homophobic aspects of many ethnic articulations of nationhood.
2. The second factor is the profound impact of the First world ethnic studies' commentary on the establishment of the postcolonial studies, which often reflects both spatial and psychic distance from Third World nations as well as a strong impulse to critique First world nationalisms.
3. The third factor is the emergence of either the reality or the discourse of globalization in which nation states are presumed to be surrounded by the circulations of global capital and the rise of new communication technology.

Paul Gilroy's book *The Black Atlantic,* juxtaposes the fatal junction of the concept of nationality with the concept of culture. According to Gilroy, this junction leads to the tragic popularity of ideas about the integrity and purity of cultures. Cultural Diasporas inspire postcolonial scholars to recognize cultural hybridity and social plurality. Current critical articulations of postcolonial Diasporas have benefited from Gilroy's work and we must recognize that Gilroy's work often seems consciously polemic and normative on the topics of nation and diaspora respectively.

The first issue of the journal *Diaspora* announces that "Diaspora is concerned with the ways in which nations, real yet imagined communities, are included, brought into being, made and unmade, in culture and politics, both on land people call their own and in exile" (and goes on to argue that) Transnational communities are sometimes the paradigmatic Other of the nation state and at other times its ally, lobby, or even, as in the case of Israel, its precursor."

A final point, we need to mention is that, just as there is no guarantee that nations are inclined towards fascism, there is also no guarantee that diasporas are socially pluralist, devoid of ethnic absolutism and brimming with postcolonial liberation.

The term Diaspora within postcolonial studies suggests not only a break in cultural politics and social justice, rather, the final stage in the ascendancy of migrant, cosmopolitan and first world metropolitan in representations of the postcolonial experience. Many postcolonial diaspora critics make the argument that diaspora provides alternatives not only to nation states but also to globalization understood as homogenizing of difference. No contemporary critic can afford to ignore the possibility that, in the global era they map out an uncomfortable collusion might emerge between proponents of Empire and proponents of what we here call the postcolonial diaspora.

In order to accomplish the goal of developing critical methodologies for work on the postcolonial diaspora, we need to appreciate the meanings, effects, and epistemologies that have historically consolidated themselves around the term diaspora, and have thereby affected the ways in which the postcolonial diaspora have initially been conceptualized.

Globalization has created complex interconnections across the world. People move across borders, travel across cities and nations, media exchanges are interlinked across the globe, cultures have acquired a mobility that brings about new civilization of clashes and struggles between people. These interchanges and encounters have produced remarkable transformation in the space of politics, economics and culture. The global movements of capital, labour, goods, people and ideas have enabled the creation of transnational space and diasporic cultures. The displacement of millions of migrant labourers, refugees and professionals from the postcolonial 'Third World' to 'First World' and the formation of numerous migrant is now one of the most important defining features of the 20th century.

There are two things that need to be analyzed: the first thing is to analyze the transformation of identities that have emerged in the transnational diaspora communities. How diasporic identities are important sites for the reconstruction of knowledge about culture, identity and practices, needs to be explored. The second thing that needs to be explored is to show how studying the practices of global cultural flows and transnational Diasporas has important implications for reconstructing knowledge about; a) the concept of culture, b) identity and self, and c) the discipline of psychology.

a) Changing Semiotics of Culture: The change in time and space has developed a complex connectivity between cultures, integration and fragmentation of communities, shifts in identity construction and new margins and centres of power are going through the process of construction. In today's postcolonial world, culture and cultural practices are not only situated in particular geographies, but are relocated in new spaces. As families and people increasingly live in multiple imagined communities, their notion of cultural locations brings different cultures into a single social field.

b) Notion of Identity: To link globalization and formation of Diasporas with culture and identity is to get insight about the broader conditions in which social life is being organized and transformed. This sense-making activity of culture provides the material for shaping identity and one's consciousness about the world. As culture inserts itself in the new contexts, we get new configurations of power and hegemony in identities that are being created at the local-global nexus.

c) Discipline of Psychology: If global context and diaspora formations have to serve as a useful analytical tool for the construction of identity in the present transnational world, then we must re-examine the specific ways in which psychology needs to move as cultural context. We think of psychology as a multi-sited imaginary that connects complex social spaces and follows the cultures as it travels through transnational networks.

Thus, migration and Diasporas cannot be separated from colonialism, because it is the historical condition of colonialism and postcoloniality that has led to the global displacement of South Asian people under various forms of migration. They also cannot be separated from the expansion of global capitalism that functions to provide mobility to these postcolonial subjects.

Work Cited

Desai, Jigna. *Beyond Bollywood: The Cultural Politics of South Asian Diasporic Films.* London: New York: Routledge, 2004.

Globalisation: Some Developments in Literature

CHRISTINE WILLIAMS
Sydney School of Arts & Humanities

Throughout most of human history, writers have written for those within their own culture. Indigenous storytellers, including those who created story in choreographed dance forms and sculptural and carved or painted patterns, have interpreted the world for their own people, those they felt close to and understood. They drew on natural beings, plants and land formations to give understanding and significance to their lives. In the villages of India, Africa, Europe, the Andes, and among the ice huts of the Inuit, the normal and the supernatural were described in action and import, given character, explained in the context of those living in their communities. The forms were various: fairy stories, folk (or common people's) tales, and philosophical or devotional teachings such as the epics, the *Ramayana* and the *Mahabharata*. Storytellers would concentrate on necessary common learning, sharing tales that warned about the dangers of volcanic eruptions and strangers, the goals of human existence, interpretations of the northern lights that swept across the arctic sky, or the symbolisation of thunder and lightning. These nominated storytellers practised their arts with the sanction of the whole community, in recognition of the need for this coming together of members who shared a common heritage and a common future. The knowledge and creativity of the storytellers was acknowledged as a valuable requirement for the well-being of the entire community—they garnered respect. The stories they told were reliable, truthful, cautionary or an explanation of the way lives might be usefully lived—or, if meant only for entertainment, full of obvious trickery and fanciful fun.

Expressions of Australian indigenous understandings of the innate link between human and other forms found in nature feature in the many indigenous stories spread across the great southern continent. Typical of these is a Western Arnhem Land story, part of an anthology of indigenous legends collected by the anthropologist Catherine Berndt in the 1970s. As the story goes, a man called Crow and his wife Black Cockatoo go walking through Djauan country to Wulduwug. They begin to feel unwell so Crow gathers stringy-bark and soft grass to cover them for warmth, and Black Cockatoo finds paperbark for a roof. Then they begin to grow feathers, and decide that rather than die and have their bodies go underground, it would be better to fly like the birds. They cover their bodies with black grass and go to sleep. By the time of the next moon, they've grown beaks and claws, changed their language for that of birds and flown far away. The couple faces the adversity of illness and it is their fate to survive through transformation. In the telling of the story no barrier to transformation is considered to exist between bird and human. (Berndt 22)

In another story, Sun Woman is a woman like all others but she makes herself a Dreaming Sun. She lives underground and is so hot and dangerous that if she were to come from the deep earth to the surface she would burn humans to ashes. She has a daughter who is also a Sun Dreaming and every morning when the birds first begin to talk, she brings light and heat to a darkened world so humans can hunt for food. Woman, Dreaming, light and heat—all are imparted with transformative powers within nature as a whole. (Berndt 17)

The Gimuy Yidinji people live by the sea near Cairns on the Great Barrier Reef, and share many legends in the form of dance. Passed down through generations for thousands of years, their dances are still performed today. As the Australian Government now acknowledges:

> There are both similarities and differences between the ways Aboriginal and Torres Strait Islander groups use the sea in their customary practices. Each group has their own distinctive culture and identity, and often within groups there are many more clans and kinship groups whose discrete characteristics further distinguish one from the other. (Australian Government 2017)

One powerful legend is that a fish was once speared by accident, and the people realised it was their sacred fish, the stingray. It became so angry it made the sea become rough and rise up over the land.

Our most current science supports that legendary dance story of uncontrollable seas rising. The Great Barrier Reef is the world's largest coral reef, and exists because of a shallow continental shelf that sits beside a sudden drop of two thousand metres to the sea floor. The shelf creates the perfect conditions for an ecosystem of algae and coral that need sunlight reaching into the sea to a depth of about 35 metres. These conditions became possible at the end of the Ice Age, about 14,000 years ago, when the coastline was inundated by rising water flowing over the land at a rate of hundreds of metres every year.

Is it only now in a world of 'globalised' communication—i.e. the information technology devices and processes that form part of the information revolution overtaking the world—that we are able to recognise the truth of that 'affinity with nature' story above. Such stories are in stark contrast to the former dominant mind-set which ruled international and inter-cultural relations based on a materialist and white moralist progress model. There have been revolutions before, and there has been globalisation, even though the sense of global reach has never been so vast (reaching into every village and hamlet in the remotest parts of the world) and the empires that administer this reach have never been so wealthy and powerful. Perhaps this far-reaching information technology revolution has come at just the right time in history, when we desperately need to share cultural stories that emphasise the dire need for the return of respect for the natural world and for that respect to be applied to save threatened species of flora and fauna. The stories we share—our literary treasury—may be the conduit for the revitalisation of our planet.

As society advanced from those early legends in the more agriculturally and then industrially advanced parts of the world, life became more complex, and so it was with writing story. More rules were set down about what might be expected within a particular literary form. Fairy stories warned children to follow strangers in a pipe dance at their peril—not to trust a wolf in grandmother's clothing. The length of stories was determined by the attention span of the children who heard the tales. Short stories for adults told of the vagaries and sadness of life. Some poems were epic and tested recitation skills through strength of mind.

The development of the prose novel in Western Europe along with short story forms was derived from the stories of classical Greece such as Homer's *Iliad* and *Odyssey* (800-700 B.C.) which later informed the minds of the ancient Roman authors, Cicero, Virgil, Ovid and Horace, who wrote in a wide range of forms: essays, histories, poems including love lyrics, plays, and other writing such as obituaries and inscriptions.

The romance story genre predated the rise of the realist novel but is a closely related long prose narrative. Literary historian Susan Manning says Sir Walter Scott's "historical intelligence comprehended an enquiry into the relation of history to legend, which neither dismissed 'folklore' nor ultimately lent it credence." She says 'reality' in Scott's Waverley novels "emerges as a composite construed from different perspectives of belief." Rational and supernatural explanations for historical events sit side by side in his work, she says, and "traditional wisdom, like romance, supplemented the experience of the past offered by narrative history." He had "a life-long interest in melding folk experience into the rational literary forms of civil society," Manning believed. (148)

Scott defined the romance as "a fictitious narrative in prose or verse; the interest of which turns upon marvellous and uncommon incidents," whereas in the novel "the events are accommodated to the ordinary train of human events and the modern state of society," according to Susan Manning. (xxv) With increasing 'civilisation' and its emphasis on urbanisation there was evidently a concomitant diminution in natural habitat as subject matter for storytelling in the novel form.

The novel is now defined as a long, fictional narrative, chronological or at least sequential, and usually in prose, that describes intimate human experiences. Cervantes's story *Don Quixote* (1605) is often cited as the first modern novel, while other theorists such as Ian Watt say the novel was born in its modern form based on 'realism' in the 18th century, espoused by the French Realists as distinct from previous 'romance' stories and historical accounts through its acuity in showing heroes (and heroines) with human foibles or weaknesses. (Watt 9)

According to Watt, "the realism of the novels of Defoe, Richardson and Fielding is closely associated with the fact that Moll Flanders is a thief, Pamela a hypocrite, and Tom Jones a fornicator"; the novel "attempts to portray all the varieties of human experience" (11). The American novelist Jonathan Franzen has described the novel 'as primarily a liberal form' since it arose with liberal democracy. (JF http:// mpegmedia.abc.net.au/rn/podcast/2016/12/bay_20161230_1005.mp3). And it is argued that the novel reached its zenith in the 19th century with *Wuthering Heights* (Emily Bronte), *Jane Eyre* (Charlotte Bronte), *Middlemarch* (George Eliot), *Frankenstein* (Mary Shelley), *Tess of the d'Urbervilles* (Thomas Hardy), *Pride & Prejudice* (Jane Austen), and the fourteen novels of Charles Dickens.

Today there are fears that the novel with its richness and insight into the human condition is dying as a form due to its length and unsuitability to the supposed short attention spans of readers in the internet age.

We're certainly going through a globalisation of the English language, which borrows from other languages and loses much of its own distinct and localised vernacular in the process. The changes are due principally to the unpredictability of economic pressures in the market and social and economic pressures to conform and appeal to readers potentially worldwide. Not only is there a globalisation of our language under way but also a globalisation—with uncertain outcomes—of our literature born of our language.

Australia has lost most indigenous languages as they were spoken in communities in the 18th, 19th and 20th centuries, and with these languages their cache of stories. And in the first decade and a half of the 21st century we're also losing or have lost vocabulary which has persisted for two hundred years since white occupation of the country, many words derived from the rhyming slang of Cockney East Enders or the from the quirky sayings or myths of the counties that our immigrants—free or convict—hailed from. Words fading from the Australian vernacular include 'cobber' and 'bloke' (meaning men, familiarly), a 'sheila' (a woman), a 'boofhead' (a stupid person), 'go to billyo' (now, 'get lost'), a 'galah' (a native parrot, meaning a silly person), 'down the gurgler' (disappeared), 'gone to blazes' (gone to hell), 'bonza' (meaning excellent, whereas now 'sick'—or 'deadly' from indigenous parlance—might be used by young people to describe excellence). These former colourful words are fast disappearing from our slang as their users age and die.

In the meantime, the home-grown Australian dictionary 'Macquarie' in its most recent update has included the Americanism 'fake news,' and straight from the internet, 'filter bubble' (meaning search engines building a user's personal preferences), and 'alt-right' (meaning extremely right wing), as well as 'halal snack pack,' which recognises the influence of Middle Eastern food on our daily lives and language. Even the spelling of 'gaol' has changed to 'jail' to conform to American spelling, as most Australians now don't recognise the archaic spelling. In any case this should improve saleability of texts to an American readership, part of the inevitable invasion by the U.S. empire into our culture and language. The fear is that authors worldwide are contributing to a long-term narrowing of vocabulary and writing creativity in order to conform to United States standards.

In the midst of what is declared to be an almost infinite capacity to sell literary wares globally, there exists the uncomfortable fact that authors and publishers have to moderate regional language differences and compete among hundreds of thousands, sometimes millions, of similarly hopeful authors largely poorly educated in both storytelling and marketing. Now let loose on the internet, and specifically Amazon, which accounts for two-thirds of all ebook sales, how are these single self-publishing authors, especially, going to be found by potential consumers?

That question doesn't stop writers from attempting to conquer the world in the midst of specific, often hidden, rules about how to attract the attention of readers. For example, many bloggers may receive the following mixed blessing-or-curse advice on the back-end of their blogsites, exhorting them to address each of these points in order to lift a story's visibility to Google search engines.

- "No meta description has been specified, search engines will display copy from the page instead." [If you don't write your own meta description or synopsis, the automated service will do it for you. And correct punctuation seems of little importance by the Google writer.]
- "Bad SEO score: No images appear in this page, consider adding some as appropriate." [Words are increasingly considered insufficient to tell a story online these days.]

- "OK SEO score: The slug for this page contains stop words, consider removing them." [Stop words are small words such as 'a,' 'an,' 'the,' and 'but' that might interfere with the fast delivery of a brief headline or 'slug' to internet networks—yet they might be essential to meaning.]
- "OK SEO score: No links appear in this page, consider adding some as appropriate." [Links to other sites are encouraged yet it may not be in an author's interest to offer a distraction for a reader to quickly opt out of his/her article.]
- "OK SEO score: The SEO title contains the focus keyword, but it does not appear at the beginning; try and move it to the beginning." [Again, this is a direction that might not serve the author's sentence purpose.]
- "Good SEO score: The focus keyword appears in the first paragraph of the copy." [Murder may be the focus of a murder mystery but it wouldn't necessarily be good writing to use the word 'murder' in the first paragraph.]
- "Good SEO score: The keyword density is 1%, which is great; the focus keyword was found 6 times." [Is this really the way an author wants to be encouraged to write—by repeating a word 6 times within a few paragraphs?]
- "Good SEO score: The text contains 597 words. This is more than or equal to the recommended minimum of 300 words." [Even recommendations for the minimum word length for an article!]
- "Good SEO score: The page title has a nice length." [Yet surely titles should be decided on meaning rather than their length being "nice."]
- "Good SEO score: You've never used this focus keyword before, very good." [And finally, praise for using a new word in the title of an article, without consideration for whether it's even relevant to the story.]

The Google guidelines are detailed and certainly shape the presentation of stories on blogs. There's discouragement in the use of "stop" words, many of which used to be called "articles" or "conjunctions" and had a distinct purpose in clarifying meaning in a text. This discouragement is a clear example of how inhibitive the shaping has become and how writing in English may be adversely affected over the longer-term.

In the use of English as a second language, the words 'a' and 'the' are often interchangeable or left out completely—a usage that is not acceptable to speakers of English as their first tongue. With a significant rise in numbers of speakers of English as a second language, it begs the question whether previously distinct national dialects of English might finally be merged, and further, whether such a move would mean clearer communication or more confusion? For example, it is common usage in India to use the words "isn't it?" at the end of many sentences which do not use the verb "to be." Maybe this usage one day becomes common all over the English-speaking world? English has proven an adaptive and constantly evolving language, so a lessening of the opprobrium directed against the ungrammatical use of 'isn't it?' by grammar purists is entirely possible.

What have we created today, with millions of self-published authors plying their wares on Amazon and Kindle while an increasingly diminished literary elite looks down upon the writing of the *hoi polloi* from a hallowed height? Now we have a plethora of self-appointed writers who generate story from a range of motives—especially that of wealth-and-fame-seeking. Literary democratisation soon may be the undoing of deeply considered writing itself. My thoughts are that if the novel disappears from contemporary publication lists and remains as a relic of sympathies and cultural affinities of a bygone age, the poem may rise to take its place . . . a work of simple though often nuanced presentation with the capacity to convey deep understanding of human nature and activity.

There's a mismatch in statistics between quality discernment of texts and indiscriminate consumption, broadly across all national book markets, as ever there has been. The sale of print books is in the doldrums of low percentage despite rising population figures, and also despite the clamorous claims that people are now turning away from electronic books back to print. (Dudley-Nicholson)

What is clearly evident is that short forms of literature are dominating the world of the internet, that space which occupies most readers' attentions day in, day out: the screen, whether it be the mobile/ cell/ smart phone, the iPad or tablet, the laptop, desktop computer or on an amalgam of dedicated TV and video flat screen. The easiest and quickest way to take a dose of literature is via the latest formats or forms. These constitute flash fiction, an umbrella term used to describe any fictional work of extreme brevity, including the six-word story, or the 140-character story, also known as twitterature, or another form called the 'dribble' (50 words), the 'drabble' (100 words)—even though the English novelist Margaret Drabble herself was not known to indulge in such concise stories—and sudden fiction (750 words). The term 55 Fiction is a variant of the 'drabble,' with Wikipedia offering the following criteria for the 55 Fiction 'literary' forms:

1. 55 words or fewer, however some publishers actually require exactly 55 words—no more and no less;
2. A setting;
3. One or more characters;
4. Some conflict; and
5. A resolution. (*Not limited to the moral of the story*)

The question as to whether the title of the story is or is not part of the overall word count is debatable, depending on the publisher, but is said not to be allowed to exceed seven words.

And where is this fiction predominantly to be found? That nebulous space, 'online,' where anything goes, where rules are being set instantly and informally and overturned almost as quickly.

Beyond the flash fiction cited above, we continue to value the traditional short story form, ranging from 1,500 to 30,000 words, with a long short story maybe 10,000 words. Novellas run at around 20,000 to 50,000 words and novels range from 55,000 to 150,000, with the extreme upper end reaching 200,000 to 300,000 words—very rare and almost impossible to market. The most highly acclaimed art form is the novel, because of the difficulty of writing a work with simultaneous strands of narrative, a major plot with sub-plots, and which vaults beyond the simplicity of writing a story which deals essentially with one or at most a few characters or just episodes in their fictional lives, as occurs in a short story. The novella may soon usurp the place of the novel in popularity given that it is much more possible to read the complete story of a novella at one sitting rather than that of a novel.

And a refreshing turn being increasingly taken by many highly regarded authors is 'doing it for themselves.' For instance, Margaret Atwood has admitted publicly her promiscuous flirting with Wattpad while still accepting publishers' offers.

> 'But Margaret,' you can hear them whispering [she writes]. 'You're a literary icon at the height of your powers; it says so on your book covers. Why are you sneaking out with an online story-sharing site heavy on romance, vampires and werewolves? You should be endorsing Literature, capital L. Get back up on that pedestal! Strike a serious pose! Turn to stone!'

Atwood believes that the internet is boosting literacy and likes the way you can use any IT device to post your own writing.

> No one need know how old you are, what your social background is, or where you live. Your readers can be anywhere. And if you're worried about adverse reactions . . . you can use a pseudonym. You can be FlamingLeprechaun and represent yourself with a picture of a bat or a spoon: the internet lends itself to surrealism. Then you can post stories about Pod People or affairs with smouldering hunks undead for 2,000 years, which beats 'My Summer Holiday'

> every time. Not only that, you'll have readers who leave encouraging comments on your message board, thus boosting your morale.

And it's thought by some that long form writing is not so much disappearing as evolving into series publication on sites such as Inkitt, Radish and Channilo, just like in the days of serialization of Dickens' works. Is the internet actually offering the best of both worlds—literary quality as well as smart spontaneous quick wit?

It seems that the internet bends to the wishes of the most vocal, and criteria can be changed without the sonorous sounds of professors ahh-ing and ahem-ing as they judge the best efforts of students they are shaping—for careers in literature-production or literature-critiquing or for the dismal life of an unfulfilled writer (a non-writer) who has been rejected by any number of traditional publishers. The egos of these rejects have at last risen up, to the point where now anyone who has self-published a story between six and 750 words may call herself or himself a writer. Or even 'an author,' which in the past has indicated publication as against simply having written stories and tried to sell them. Where now are the bounds of definition? With self-publishing, vanity publishing, small publishing, arthouse publishing, boutique publishing and traditional mainstream publishing, a job in academia is still not determined entirely on traditional 'publishability'—since there are scholarly qualifications that need to be satisfied in the eyes of the keepers of the flame of literature.

On the question of self-assessment of talent to which the academic establishment objects, 'Vain and glorious in print?' was the title of a question this author raised about vanity publishing in a column in *Australian Book Review* in 1998, referring to the fact that peer review is a side issue for fine vignerons and cheesemakers who rely principally on market taste, selling directly to the public to determine their social acceptance. So why shouldn't writers? It was a radical idea then and remains so among university elites, most of whom don't like to sully their eyes by reading the work of JK Rowling or Dan Brown, among the most popular authors in the world. (Williams 58)

Almost twenty years later there's no shame in self-publishing though being chosen by one's literary peers or superiors is preferable—both practically and in terms of status. Publication by other than self shows that you've been accepted by astute critics or publishers who want to make money from your work, whereas self-publication is merely an empty statement of a belief in your own work. Internet 'writers'—whether self-publishing ebook authors or blog writers or traditionally published authors—are spilling over the barriers to recognition that academics, literary agents and publishing houses have long upheld against the ambitious untalented hordes. Elites similar to certain political opportunists in the United States have been in favour of building fences to keep out the non-Anglo-Saxon, non-white people they consider inferior to themselves, having forgotten or never known one of the greatest poems most representative of the benefits of the immigrant melting pot quality of the 'united' states, Robert Frost's 'Mending Wall':

> Before I built a wall I'd ask to know
> What I was walling in or walling out,
> And to whom I was like to give offence.
> Something there is that doesn't love a wall,
> That wants it down.

I come again to the question of forms of writing and the concept of 'high literary quality.' What is literature as distinct from writing? Why do certain works hold sway for centuries and others drift into extinction? A best-selling writer from one decade may be passed over the next, and become completely unknown by 99% of the reading public within 50 years, as was the case for William Blake, Bill Blake that is, the husband of the acclaimed international writer, Christina Stead. He produced New York bestsellers in the 1940s but it is his wife who still holds a leading place in the pantheon of Australia's most respected novelists. Franzen, a fan of Stead, says her novel *The Man Who Loved Children* is an important book for the reason that it shows that one "can write at that level of psychological violence" and the book "can still be fun, or humorous." (Franzen) What are the elements that are used to judge not only high literary quality but longevity in the popularity stakes over decades and even centuries? Who of the current crop of literary 'It' girls and 'It' boys will still be remembered by 2050?

Christina Stead thought those who referred to high literary quality were pretentious. Effectiveness was what she imbued into her stories. Writing to produce an emotional effect on the reader, which is an inexact science. Originality of ideas and expression are prized and one doesn't need the novel length to attain them. We've entered a new age where brevity of story is also an asset.

Globalisation is upon us and much is made of how valuable a tool it is for the education and liberation of an individual's mind. Anyone who can read in at least one language is enabled access to literatures of the world through translating services on the internet. Similarly, a writer can pick and choose what to use from the array of languages and ideas of many cultures in the creation of new texts culturally apposite to her or his own.

It might be alarming to consider that the internet supplies more thought and writing detritus to the mass of humankind than individually we feel we can cope with on a daily basis. But it does have the advantage of being the great leveller. So we needn't feel obliged to label texts either as having 'hlq' or base lowest common denominator value. Better to think in terms of utility: this text is informational, another text has evocative poetic imagery of the natural world, while yet another makes a point about social class.

I'd like to refer to several more fictional examples to bear out my contention that despite those texts that are referred to as tweets, pithy, often emotional, and overused by some self-serving politicians, the international network of IT screen formats can serve to liberate us all in some way or other. In the 'First World West' we so often act as individuals and our literature reflects that independence of mind. But we are generally more likely to act as individuals in how we have sex and with whom, whether we marry at all, what choices we make in employment (for those of us who can find full-time jobs), the level of education we want to pursue, the degree of outspokenness we have with friends and family, and our choices in reading and writing.

In secular Australia it comes as a shock that most young people in India are held to abide by age-old religious or social traditions such as arranged marriages, a horrifying consideration in our liberal society. In India, social inhibition and social constriction hold sway in so many respects—restriction through religious beliefs and enforcement through social shaming, restriction through hierarchy in employment, social ostracism through poverty or caste and its opposite, caste upheaval. It can even operate in some states more than others in the power of matriarchy, and the belief in the sanctity of family—the natural domain for women to exert their power—with the continuation of the family often viewed as more important than the need for individual education and personal growth. Australians might read a novel about the quaint idiosyncrasies of family repression such as those shown in Vikram Seth's *A Suitable Boy*—or *A Suitable Girl,* primed to grace our bookshelves possibly this year—without actually realising that in the 21st century arranged marriages are a strong active social determinant still. So, in that situation the power of literature to make a point, to have a purpose in educating us all to the differences and dilemmas between East and West, might be in vain if we as readers do not fully comprehend the implacable differences in social mores between many varying cultures, as we read from within the safety of our own more liberal society.

Yet considering cultural proscriptions and social exclusivities is not entirely helpful in reviewing the influence of texts read beyond their homeland borders. In his editor's Introduction to the compilation, *Modern Indian Literature*, Amit Chaudhuri points to many commonalities between Indian and Western literature.

> A cursory glance at the ancient and modern literary traditions of India—one thinks even of translations such as Ramanujan's English rendering of ancient Tamil poetry or Arvind Mehrotra's versions of Prakrit love poetry—will confirm that delicacy and nuance are not the prerogative of the rational, bourgeois West alone, but are central to, and manifested with great skill and beauty in, all significant examples of Indian writing. . . . While there are many differences between the traditional Indian epic and the postcolonial Indian English novel, one seems to be of particular importance; the mythic imagination from which those epics sprang was disturbingly amoral and estranging . . . and it is from this amorality that the epics reveal to us the mystery of human nature and the universe. The postcolonial novel, on the other hand, is often rooted in the liberal middle-class conscience and founded in the liberal humanist verities: multiculturalism is good; colonialism and fundamentalism are bad, etc. (xxv, xxvi)

By contrast, as mentioned earlier, among the disadvantages in sharing literary texts with writers from other cultures is that we often misunderstand the degrees of inhibition that apply to writers from within their own cultures. From all of our interactions via the internet and face to face, we pick up stereotypes, and for Australians thinking about India these often revolve around money, drugs, sex, sport and spirituality—which are Australians' own predilections. For example, the title of the anthology *Of Sadhus and Spinners* oozes stereotype but delivers fresh views. Contributing to the collection of stories compiled in 2009 with the assistance of the Australia-India Council, several authors take up these stereotypes with the purpose of breaking them down.

In 'A Democrat on the Ganges,' Australia's late great historian, Manning Clark, plays with the stereotypes of many Indians' excuse of national poverty to act cannily in financial transactions, from street beggar up, and many Australians' resentments about the interactions. The character Jack Howell prides himself on his sense of democracy and his heterosexual masculinity, and doesn't want to be taken for a fool. Yet he finds by the end of the story there's no getting around it. When in India, do as the Indians. (Clark 47-54)

In another story from the collection, 'A Foot in the Stream,' David Malouf creditably attempts to describe the great expanse of humanity on the move that greets the first-time visitor to a country of 1.2 billion people.

> In lamplit shanties, in a haze of wood-smoke, and dust, men were tapping away at metal or scouring great copper dishes and pots. In other places, in the manner of all Third World countries, mysterious things were being done with car tyres and inner tubes; motorbikes and cars were being worked on, all the parts laid out beside the road while mechanics in greasy overalls, or in shabby native dress, squatted or lay with their feet sticking out into the traffic. Naked children splashed in puddles. Pedlars spread their wares on a bit of carpet. Pigs rooted in garbage, cows wandered. It was all very dense and confusing. . . .
>
> This promiscuousness of India, its teeming plenitude, far from being oppressive, seems invigorating. It humbles but lifts the spirit. It seems immemorial, endless, indestructible. Things have been like this forever, and will go on like this, in defiance of every catastrophe, into a future too remote to contemplate. We will survive here, we humans, one species among many—that is what India promises. (142, 146)

The late Vicki Viidikas tackled the drugs and spirituality themes of the anthology in her own bohemian way in 'The Clothesline in the Himalayas':

> And it was good to feel that close to the sky, to understand why the monasteries should be built among such mountains, to speculate on . . . Lord Shiva himself who sat in the Himalayas and meditated for seven years. . . .
>
> Bear and I would come back silent from those morning walks, lugging our mortal hearts and empty stomachs, and collapse in our tiny room. Satisfied. Amazed. And when the clothesline was smoked, Bear started on the string carpet; by the time we left it was five inches shorter. (Viidikas 101)

In 'Maisie Goes to India,' Joan London wrote about what every traveller seeks, 'paradise':

> The Indians will never change,' said Noel. 'It's their religion. They call their time on earth their karma. The earth is a place of cruelty and sorrow. Each time the aim is to become a little more free. The lighter one becomes the happier one is.'
>
> 'Until it's Paradise on earth,' said Maisie to him.
>
> 'Paradise is when one doesn't come back at all.'
>
> 'But who wants to leave?' cried Padre Lewis. 'Paradise is when a chap is surrounded by members of the fairer sex.'
>
> 'Earthly pleasures, Padre!'
>
> 'Mere appreciation of God's beauty in the world, dear boy.' His paper crown had slipped over one ear.
>
> 'Paradise is what you think might happen,' said Mona, 'and never does.'
>
> 'Paradise,' said Noel, 'is when you're satisfied.' (175)

There are ways that global literature can be most effective and those are in demonstrating through story the values that we can share and which can create an impact in bringing about change for human relationship and also for the benefit of our common natural world, our planet. Our common paradise. This is an understanding that the novelist Arundhati Roy has brought to her political and environmental writing since her first great novel,

The God of Small Things, in writing about the paternalism and hypocrisy of the Indian government in pushing for the construction of massive dam and irrigation projects at the cost of poor local residents and the natural environment. (1999a, 1999b)

The destruction or protection of our environment is a common theme that is ageless, running through indigenous people's stories from time immemorial to the present. The sanctity of water, for instance, is recognised in different ways in different cultures. In Australia's northern state, Queensland, there's an indigenous story associated with prominent landmarks and settlements on what is known as the Sunshine Coast. A local legend tells how Ninderry, a rival from another clan, steals a young woman named Maroochy from Coolum, whom he was to marry. When Coolum rescues her by stealth, Ninderry chases them and knocks off Coolum's head, which rolls into the sea and is today called Mudjimba Island. His body is represented by Mount Coolum. For his treacherous attack, Ninderry is also turned by the gods into stone, as a cluster of hills is named after him. Maroochy flees inland where she weeps so copiously that her tears flow down the mountain to form the Maroochy River. (Sunshine Coast Council)

In his novel, *The Hungry Tide*, Amitav Ghosh takes another river delta, the Sundarban, as a fecund setting for a big story of the blending of culture and romance using image-making based on the mangrove tidal forest where salt and fresh waters mingle. He draws on an age-old image from what the narrator calls a Bengali script:

> In our legends it is said that the goddess Ganga's descent from the heavens would have split the earth had Lord Shiva not tamed her torrent by tying it into his ash-smeared locks. To hear this story is to see the river in a certain way: as a heavenly braid, for instance, an immense rope of water, unfurling through a wide and thirsty plain. That there is a further twist to the tale becomes apparent only in the final stages of the river's journey—and this part of the

> story always comes as a surprise, because it is never told and thus never imagined. It is this: there is a point at which the braid comes undone; where Lord Shiva's matted hair is washed apart into a vast, knotted tangle. Once past this point the river throws off its bindings and separates into hundreds, maybe thousands, of tangled strands. . . . The islands are the trailing threads of India's fabric, the ragged fringe of her sari. (6)

Perhaps we might also take this image as the individuation that is possible in literature being disseminated instantly through globalisation. Writers may offer up their individual stories freed from the bonds of repressed and repressing families and communities, outdated social systems and exploitative power hierarchies, to unite with other islands of individuality seeking to share through literature, simultaneously locally and globally, an appreciation of human intimacy and interaction, just one part of the complexity and splendour of our natural environment.

Bibliography

Attenborough, David. http://iview.abc.net.au/programs/david-attenboroughs-great-barrier-reef/ZW0220A001S00

Atwood, Margaret (2012). Why Wattpad Works. https://www.theguardian.com/books/2012/jul/06/margaret-atwood-wattpad-online-writing

Australian Government (2017). Great Barrier Reef Marine Park Authority http://www.gbrmpa.gov.au/our-partners/traditional-owners/traditional-owners-of-the-great-barrier-reef

Berndt, Catherine H. (1979). *Land of the Rainbow Snake: Aboriginal Children's Stories and Songs from Western Arnhem Land*. Sydney: Collins.

Chaudhuri, Amit, ed. (2016) *Modern Indian Literature*. London: Picador.

Chekhov, Anton (1951). "The Seagull." *Plays*. London: Penguin.

Clark, Manning (2009). "A Democrat on the Ganges." *Of Sadhus and Spinners*. Noida: HarperCollins India.

Dudley-Nicholson, Jennifer (2017). Print's charming: paper books are staging a comeback as e-book sales fall worldwide. http://www.

news.com.au/technology/prints-charming-paper-books-are-staging-a-comeback-as-ebook-sales-fall-worldwide/news-story/335a5a9b4 2823 a4281763b36cd13420e

Franzen, Jonathan (2016). Jonathan Franzen in conversation. ABC Radio National. http://mpegmedia.abc.net.au/rn/podcast/2016/12/bay _20161230_1005.mp3

Frost, Robert (1914). "Mending Wall." https://m.poets.org/poetsorg/poem/mending-wall

Ghosh, Amitav (2009). *The Hungry Tide*. London: HarperCollins.

Joyce, James (1993). "Araby." *Dubliners*. Hertfordshire: Wordsworth.

London, Joan (2009). "Maisie Goes to India." *Of Sadhus and Spinners.*

Malouf, David (2009). "A Foot in the Stream." *Ibid.*

Manning, Susan, ed. (1992). "Essay on Romance." *Prose Works* volume vi, 129, in Introduction to Walter Scott's *Quentin Durward.* Oxford: Oxford University Press. https://books.google.com.au/books?id=Lq5BmYVvRtcC&pg=PA148&lpg=PA148&dq=Manning,+Susan+(ed.)+%22Essay+on+ Romance%22,&source=bl&ots=_28wSoNQwA&sig=cw1mx4ZkzQYaBICRVVatdvKYQxo&hl=en&sa=X&ved=0ahUKEwjjkvfMhfr RAhWCJpQKHaJYCMgQ6AEIGTAA#v=onepage&q=Manning%2C%20Susan%20(ed.)%20%22Essay%20on%20Romance% 22%2C&f=false

O. Henry (2002). "The Furnished Room." *O. Henry Stories*. London: The Folio Society.

Roy, Arundhati (1999a). *The Cost of Living*. New York: Modern Library.

_____ (1999b). 'The Greater Common Good,' *Outlook Magazine* 24 May. http://www.outlookindia.com/magazine/story/the-greater-common-good/207509

Sunshine Coast Council 2016 'A Dreamtime Legend,' 16 December. https://library.sunshinecoast.qld.gov.au/Heritage/History-by-Locality/Black-Swan-Park/Local-Indigenous-Heritage

Stead, Christina (2001). *The Man Who Loved Children*. London: Picador.

Watt, Ian (1957). *Realism and the Novel Form.* Los Angeles: University of California.

Williams, Christine (1998) "Rolling Colum." *Australian Book Review,* April, 58.

A Postcolonial Observation on the Bilingual Nature of Manju Kapur's *Difficult Daughters*

SHRUTI ROY CHAKRABORTI
D.B.P.M. College for Women, Secunderabad

Manju Kapur's debut novel *Difficult Daughters* published in 1998 is a well imagined, fluidly written, captivating literary work, which was awarded the Commonwealth Writers' Prize for the Best First Book. An intriguing tale of a mother recounted by her daughter is the central thought of the novel, set with the Partition as its background. The plot is well woven and all its complexities are well expressed through lucid language. It is a story of a daughter's journey to her mother's past. Ida, Virmati's daughter, traces her mother's life to find out that the physical journey ultimately led her to an inner exploration of her mother's psyche as well. Virmati had got married to Harish, a professor who was already married. As a result of this so-called blasphemous act she lost her family. This rebellious act was committed by Virmati out of a yearning for identity of a woman, in the male-dominated society more than just falling in love with a man. She was not the only difficult daughter, but Ida too was, as she was also a childless divorcee.

The novel excels as a forceful expression of Indian feminism, and examines the problems faced by women as women in the patriarchal regime. But beside its brilliant narrative, the novel has another intrinsic quality, i.e. the use of bilingual vocabulary. The merit of the novel lies in the bilingual nature of its diction, and thus establishes it as a potent Commonwealth text. Kapur's English highly deviates from the Queen's English and includes itself amongst the "other Englishes," of which Indian English is a prominent wing. This paper aims at discovering the aims and objectives of the extent of trans-creation or Indianization exercised by Kapur in *Difficult Daughters*, and also exploring the new Indian English idiom fashioned by her.

To begin the argument, I would like to refer to the preface to *Kanthapura*, where Raja Rao states, "English is not really an alien language to us. It is the language of our intellectual make-up. . . . We are all instinctively bilingual, many of us in our own language and in English. We cannot write like the English. We should not." He further comments, "The tempo of Indian life must be infused into our English expression." Although *Difficult Daughters* has been written quite some years after *Kanthapura*, but Rao's observation on the Indian writer's English is still very much contemporary and relevant regarding this novel. A further elucidation can be sought in C. Rollason's thought on the Indian English writers. Rollason in his essay "Indian Writing in English: Some Language Issues and Translation Problem," tries to point out at an unceasing yet creative tension that exists between the medium, i.e. English language and the content, i.e. the Indian mind. English language becomes the veneer in the hands of the Indian English writers, under which lies the profound Indian mind. Kapur's novel gives vent to the emotions in this mind through the stylistic charm of its vocabulary. In fact, the novel becomes highly lucid and readable only because of this Indianization of the language. It is interspersed with occurrences of Hindi and Punjabi words, loan translation, code-mixing and code switching. Kapur makes her characters express themselves using a wide range of colloquial Punjabi, and attributes her creativity a wonderful cultural context. The English becomes localized, which may remind us of Frantz Fanon's tripartite scheme or "panorama on three levels." Though Fanon's concept is essentially related to anti-colonial struggle, still a connection with the realm of Commonwealth literature can aptly be sought. Regarding the native intellectuals, Fanon comments: "after having tried to lose himself in the people . . . will on the contrary shake the people." Patricia Waugh's interpretation of this statement is: "the native intellectual learns to re-exercise agency and retrieve a self-hood that was damaged under the colonial oppression." Fanon further focuses on the native intellectual's attempt at the "reconstitution of identity through the reclamation of local cultural traditions." In Kapur's novel, the language expressing the 'local cultural traditions' or the ethos of the Punjabi community becomes the medium of retaliating the colonizer's language, or in a broader sense the colonizer's power and domination. This paper makes a humble effort to assess the role of the Indianized vocabulary in posing a challenge to the Queen's English.

Whenever an Indian writer, whose native language is not English, writes in English, he tends to reflect the impact that the L1 or mother tongue wields on his/ her creativity. As Manju Kapur is a Punjabi herself, the rampant use of Punjabi diction in her novel gives flow to her thoughts, and the confidence and dimensions of her interior aspects find a spontaneous expression.

Certain excerpts from the novel will point out at the novelty of framing of the bilingual diction. The novel begins with Ida's recollection of Virmati's death, where she says referring to what her mother says: "And, she went on, when I die I want no *shor-shar*. I don't want a *chauth*, I don't want *an uthala*, I want no one called, no one informed." The words in italics belong to Punjabi dialect, and are far removed from the Standard British English; they refer to certain rites and rituals performed in North India after a person expires. Similarly we find words related to cuisine, when Ida undertakes a train journey to Virmati's native place: "The train has not yet moved out of the station, but the women squashed next to me in this second-class ladies' compartment are already producing vast quantities of food, *puris* and *parathas* wrapped in Britannia-bread waxed paper, *aalu ki sabzi* in *mithai* boxes, mango pickle, lemon pickle, little packets of chopped onion and cucumber."

Later in the novel, when Virmati's story is narrated, we find a reference to her mother Kasturi's wedding: "Some of the *barat* intended to stay at least a week because they meant to make a holiday of the whole expedition."

As mentioned earlier the italicized words are non-English, but what is more significant is that these words and numerous more which are spread throughout the novel, are not only a linguistic expression, but a representation of a cultural ethos.

Now I would like to draw readers' attention to what becomes pretty discernible from this extensive use of Hindi and Punjabi words. First, Kapur has derived these words from varied areas of experiences, to give expression to multitude of incidents and situation throughout the novel. Second, looking at most of the words we can find that they have their English counterparts, e.g. *angan*=courtyard, *shaan*=pride, *rivaz*=tradition, *thali*=plate, *gullies*=lanes and so on, still Kapur has preferred to retain the non-English versions of these words.

Third, the inclusion of these words creates a visual impact on the Indian readers, and they keep feeling more comfortable at reading the novel, whereas any non-Indian, who is not acquainted with the culture of India, will encounter it with a sense of alienation.

Fourth, although these words have their English counterparts, and the writing would have become more perfectly English had the novelist included them, but certainly the narrative would lose its Indianness. Especially the use of the words related to food, and other social rituals like marriage and funeral have been highly instrumental in offering the novel a flavour of the 'local.'

As postcolonial literature aims to reflect the decolonization of the mind, an initiative to promote the cultural natural aesthetics has been found, invigorated by the new sense of nationalism of the former colonies. This trait has developed keeping the pace with the progression of decolonization in the 20th century, which strives at blending the national, cultural identity with the dominant aesthetics of the colonizers. Kapur's novel seems to explore this tendency to display the decolonization of the self. It is an attempt to break free from the Queen's English. The amalgamation of the English and non-English diction that has taken place in her novel claims to establish a close connection with what Mikhail Bakhtin calls 'outsideness' (uzhivanie). By the term 'outsideness,' Bakhtin refers to a "kind of creative understanding that retains its sense of space, time, and culture" and in the course of that an identity can be shaped by the simulation process of language. An essentially Indian cultural identity finds its expression through Kapur's use of bilingual diction.

The entire perspective of the novel has two-fold manifestation: First, that it attempts to subvert the hegemony that English extends on other languages throughout the world; second, the novelist intends to transform the global language to a glocal one, by accumulating multitudinous non-English/ native words within the paradigm of the Queen's English. Thus we can say that *Difficult Daughters* becomes conspicuous not only for its thematic narrative, but also for its linguistic narrative.

Works Cited

Das, Bijay Kumar. *Critical Essays on Post-Colonial Literature*. New Delhi: Atlantic, 2012.

Kapur, Manju. *Difficult Daughters*. UK: Faber and Faber, 1998.

Roy, Manju. "Language and Style in Manju Kapur's *Difficult Daughters*." IRWLE, Vol. 6, No. 1, January 2010.

Waugh, Patricia. *Literary Theory and Criticism*. New Delhi: Oxford University Press, 2013.

Colonizing the Cultural Space: An Unfurling of the Veils of Cultural Custodians for the East

V.U AMEERA
M.E.S. College, Ponnani, Malappuram Dist
FAZAL GHAFOOR
MES Medical College, Perinthalmanna, Malappuram Dist

> They cannot represent themselves; they must be represented
> Karl Marx, *The Eighteenth Brumaire of Louis Bonaparte*

A hegemonic discourse, which served the ideological underpinning for European colonizing process, Orientalism has taken new dimensions, though not deviating much from its prime purpose of establishing economic, political and cultural sway over the 'demons' of East. The nineteenth century occident writers played a pivotal role in perpetuating the western concept of Orient as the setting yearning for redemption and emancipation by the Westerners.

Orientalism can be considered in a way an offshoot of the ideology of colonialism and that the ongoing practice of 'othering' is a distinguishing aspect of colonial discourse, which is easily perceptible in Western feminism too. The hackneyed depiction of Muslim women by the xenophobic and the imperialistic folks has claimed a shelf of its own in the literal world. Forgetting conveniently, myriad instances of discrimination against women and violence against them in different parts of world, in different eras; orient women especially Muslim women are always portrayed as browbeaten lot, who are perpetually chained by patriarchy, steeped in ignorance and in abject need of liberation by Western feminists or in general by Western World.

This kind of sketchy and hazy typecasting of the East or the orient by the West or the occident is not a recent phenomenon. But these worn-out images grow to an undeniable level by a calculative employment of methodical, scientific and convincing machineries of knowledge formation that at the end it constructs a totalizing image of the other as an object of contempt. With the globalization process, Orientalism has got new dimension, with the added fuel of Islamophobia. In the early stages of Oriental studies, especially in the nineteenth century, the orient was depicted basically as monumental static culture, perceptibly different from the West, the east being depicted as exotic, feminine, irrational, emotional, despotic and basically mediocre compared to the West. Naturally, the West came to be seen as the antenna of human progress whereas the East, though cradle of greater civilizations in the past, came to be viewed as the repository of decadent values. This method of presenting the Orient opportunely justified the Europe's colonial sway over the 'second-rate' cultures.

Betty Mahmoody's memoir *Not without My Daughter* is reportedly based on the true story of Betty Mahmoody who along with her child, Mahtob was caged by her husband Moody in Iran. Apparently celebrated as a heroic saga of an American lady who made dexterous escape from the fiendish relatives of her Iranian husband, the book details the tribulations and miseries she went through in a land of barbaric and uncultured savages who assign no value to the lives of women.

While making a comparison of the rich and lively life at Detroit with the captive life of Iran, *Not without My Daughter* is a hegemonic description of Iran, which appears appalling to the civilized eyes of westerners. Deliberately hiding the ethnic fights and uprisings in Detroit during the making of this novel, Mahmoody paints Iran as if to perpetuate the Western depiction of orient as boorish and male chauvinistic and in every description, records truthfulness to the preconceived binaries that often come to the fore in the rendering of the East. The oriental reading of the book gives a homogenized representation of Iranians as backward, unrefined, primordial, fanatical and terrorist crowd who persecutes a white American lady. The filthy and unhygienic atmosphere of Iran, large sized family, practice of endogamy—everything seems outrageous to her and to the Western readers which make them depict Iran as outrageous. Even those who wear traditional attire and those who cannot speak English become the object of loathing and these serve as her criterion for shading them as bad. Through the contrastive pictures of Americans and Iranians, it validates Said's theory about creation of the other.

Evoking sympathy for a mother in a hostile land becomes a favorite theme of westerners who want to reconfirm the stereotypes about East, thus legitimizing their antagonism towards these countries. Donya Al Nahi's novel *The Heroine of the Desert* follows the heels of *Not without My Daughter,* telling the story of a woman who pawns her life to unite children snatched away from their mothers by Middle Eastern fathers who do not want them to be exposed to a liberal Western upbringing. Reclaiming her own daughter lost to a tyrannical father, she claims to have blazed a trail for others to follow.

Alexander Khan's novel, *Orphan of Islam,* hailed as the compelling story of a young boy caught between two cultures, is also set in the same mould, where the child, who is separated from his English mother, yearns to escape from the hellish Pakistan to the heavenly England. Here too, his father, just like all fathers from the Middle East turns out to be savage and merciless to their children while their white counterparts appear to be the epitomes of love and goodness. Besides, these Middle East countries are described as graves where the dreams of these young children are buried fathoms deep and where their prospects for bright future get shattered.

The post-9/11 world witnessed increasing number of books with the image of the veiled woman, which is a persuasive trope which calls upon the binary representation of third world women as enslaved, bigots, powerless and illiterate while presenting Western women as secular, liberated and individualistic. These books, sometimes life narratives, are read so as to confirm the paradigm that they need a promise that these veils can be pierced to reveal the acquiescent sexualized women who are waiting, longing and needing to be uncovered and taken. This is the classical example of the colonial fantasy, like 'the white man's burden' conception of Rudyard Kipling. The trend is definitely manifest in the current publishing sensation of Muslim women memoirs by authors such as Tara Bahrampour, Firoozeh Dumas, Norma Khouri, Leila, Azadeh Moaveni, Mukhtar Mai, Azar Nafisi, Nahid Rachlin, Marjane Satrapi, Saira Shah, and Souad. These writers have met with remarkable success, since in their testimonials they attempt to repackage the East according to the vested interests of the West. But this neo-orientalist writing often proved to be a weapon in the hands of imperialist powers for proliferation of their notion of ascendancy, rather than truly capturing the wretched plight of Middle East women.

Two popular honour killing memoirs, *Forbidden Love* by Norma Khouri and *Burned Alive: A Victim of the Law of Men* by Souad speak volumes about how white women try to orientalize the orient in the interests of perpetuating western colonial powers. These books illustrate the heroines as the sacrificial preys of the doughty Arab way of life. The texts are armchair travel books masquerading as charitable treatises. In *Forbidden Love*, Norma tells the story of her friend Dalia, whose love for the Christian soldier Michael is kept secret from her Muslim father due to religious differences. Her father ultimately finds out the truth and stabs Dalia to death, an instance of brutal honour killing. In *Burned Alive*, Souad is described as a Palestinian woman who survived an attempted murder by her brother-in-law, who soaked her with gasoline and set her on fire, as per the hideous plan of her family to do away with her for getting pregnant before marriage. She made a narrow escape to Europe with a white saviour and adopted a false name and started a family life there. The book was written as a result of repressed memory therapy, most of the works of recovered memories being found to be unreliable. These memoirs were effectively believed to be true for more than two years, though they were proved hoaxes later, because of the political post-9/11 climate revivifying orientalist attitudes about the Middle East. These sensational works use orientalist tropes and became bestselling memoirs, in the process posing many questions about how their deception was successful. These memoirs especially honour-killing memoirs, harmonious with Euro-American perspectives are intent on demonizing Islam and the policies of their home countries. Outwardly supportive of European or American foreign policy, these authors of the aforementioned works evaluate Jordanian and Palestinian culture from a purely Western standpoint, which reifies the orientalist views of their culture as backwards.

In short, these Middle Eastern women writers such as Norma Khouri, Souad, Latifah, Azar Nafisi and Ayaan Hirsi Ali, to name a few, commercialized their experiences. The production of these memoirs following the events of 9/11 marks not only the likely agency that Middle Eastern women have asserted when narrating their life stories, but conversely, the manufacturing of these memoirs can particularly permit for the global packaging of imperialist propaganda demonizing Muslim Middle Eastern countries. Thus by making demonization of others a vital principle and social median in conventional media and politics, as well as avowing that white or western societies are rational and deserving, the carnages and brutalities committed by the west are opportunely wiped away.

A popular white saviour author who is regarded as “a voice for Middle Eastern women” is the American author Jean Sassoon, best known for her Princess trilogy. Jean Sassoon has claimed to have documented the miserable condition of Saudi Arabian women which she came to know from Princess Sultana. As in all other works mentioned above, here also the clichéd presentation of women muted by the patriarchal culture of her native country and the magnanimity of her white knight in shining armour is given. Sassoon celebrates orientalized delineations of Middle Eastern Muslim women in her works. She uses the veil as the iconic figure on the cover of her biographies as if she is tackling serious issues about Muslim women lives and her publishers wrap up their texts as exotic and bona fide.

The increasing popularity gained by the writings on or by Middle East Women on their predicament shows how the Westerners want to perceive the East. But a close reading of these works provides us with the insight towards the ulterior motive behind this moral salvation the West provides and their imperial hubris. What is overriding in all of these is the vilification of local cultures as the site of actual or prospective resistance to imperial domination. To gather internal support or external legitimacy, the imperialist powers now bank on a rare breed of intellectuals to momentarily manufacture consent for their unlawful inroads into these Eastern countries. ‘Saving Brown women from Brown men,’ as Gayatri Spivak famously put it, has long been a major plank in the colonial ship since it serves to mark the colonizer as modern and civilized and provides at the same time an important reason to keep Brown men in line through practices of violence. After 9/11 attacks, this characteristic of imperial governance has been invigorated. These works have become instrumental in creating the notion that there is an urgent need of saving oriental women especially Muslim women, from their patriarchal communities, which made a cry for helping these poor victims audible, and which made the way for political domination in to oriental nations easy for the Westerners, the best instance how the mainstream white feminist groups grabbed the opportunity to articulate their support for the war in Afghanistan, claiming that US invasion would set free Afghan women. The American soldiers murdering and raping Iraqi and Afghan women not only cancels out these claims, but also points to a disturbing reality of sexual violence being integral to war and colonialism.

Bibliography

Boehmer, Elleke. "Questions of Neo-Orientalism," *Interventions* 1.1 (1998): 18-21.

Hübinette, Tobias. *Orientalism Past and Present. Tobias Hübinette.* n.d.

Huggan, Graham. "The Postcolonial Exotic," *Transitions* 64 (1994): 22-9, *JSTOR.*

Said, Edward. *Orientalism.* New York: Vintage, 1979.

Spivak, Gayatri. "Poststructuralism, Marginality, Postcoloniality and Value," *Contemporary Postcolonial Theory: A Reader*, ed. Padmini Mongia. Delhi: OUP, 1997.

Image of Women in Nisar Qabbani's Poetry

HANNAH PADMA
College of Arts and Science for Girls, Prince Sattam bin Abdulaziz University, Riyadh Province

Nizār Qabbāni is the most influential and best known Arab poet in modern times. He began composing verse while he was in school. He is considered a great protagonist of feminism in the Arab world. Besides romantic poetry, he brought forth the sufferings of womenfolk in general and of Arabs in particular. In the twentieth century Arab poetry, he became an embattled voice for change with its new visions and prophecies, and its disillusions with the very archetypal visions it has created for an Arab world, united and facing challenges of modernity. The harsh realities of every facet of Arab life, from political struggles to economic strife, compelled contemporary Arab poet's role and function to search for a dramatic arena that screams for social change. Poet's soul became a voice that is discontent with its own stagnating society, and the ruling political powers that curtailed freedom and justice, and waned in front of alienating western influences. In his poetry Nizar Qabbani has voiced the problems of Arab women. The main theme of most of his poems is love and woman. Questioned about his writings about women, Qabbani says: "They ask me: why do you write about the woman? And I answer with the utmost innocence and simplicity: And why do I not write about her?"[1] His answer to what womanhood is as follows:

> I tried to question: what is womanhood?
> Then turned away from the question

For the most important thing about womanhood is
That it is not to be told.[2]

Qabbani gives his beloved the highest place in the world of his poetry. Everything in the world follows her orders and no one can even place a leaf in its place without her permission. Her body is the most beautiful thing in the world and a source of protection, salvation and supernatural power in the face of death:

Your body is the sovereign
It rules us in the name of The Almighty
And admits us into the paradise by His permission
And drives us away from heaven by His decree. (3)

Attributing the divine power of protection to woman he says: "Nothing protects us from death except woman and writing (about her)."[4] He sees his beloved as source of influence behind all his collections. She lives in his poems and without her, his poetry would be like a body without a soul:

Thank you for your love
As it taught me reading and writing
and your beautiful face, which is hidden like a sparrow amongst
my registers and notebooks.
Thank you for living in my poems. (5)

Qabbani was an ardent feminist, an addicted and chronic lover and an enthusiastic supporter of women's rights. He says: "I do not clear myself of the crime called love. On the contrary, if someone does not fall in love, he has committed the biggest crime in the world. I say loudly that I am an addicted and chronic lover, and when there is no mistress in my life, I would be converted to blotting paper." (6) He was a ceaseless campaigner for women's rights, and his verses praise the beauty of the female body, and of love. He considered himself the champion of women's rights and harshly criticized the men who dominated society. In the following poem he has unveiled the two faces of society which are opposite to each other. He says:

Oh my Judges,
Oh my attackers
You are too cowardly to do perfect justice
You shall never frighten me. In your law
The powerful sinner wins and the unarmed is shot
A woman is questioned when she commits adultery
While compulsive adulterers are not.
The same bed they share
But only the woman falls while the man is protected.[7]

Qabbani lamented this double standard of the Arab society where daughters are discriminated against in favour of sons and sons are given the superior place at home. He says:

My brother returns from the brothel at dawn drunken
Returns as he is sultan
Who named him sultan?
And he will remain in the eyes of the family the most beautiful
and the most precious among us. (612)

Qabbani points out the discrimination meted out to woman in the following lines:

I am a woman
I am a woman
The day I came to this world
I faced the judgment of my execution
While I didn't see the door of my court
While I didn't see the face of my judges. (585)

He described his deep feelings about women and his sympathies for their deprivations and unequal treatment. He also addressed women's psychological and sociological problems and tried to make men realize that they are responsible for every wrong done to women in the Arabian society. He said in the introduction to his collection "Yawmiyātu Imraah Lā-mubāliyyah" (Diary of an indifferent woman): "This is the book of every woman . . . sentenced and executed before she could open her mouth. The East needs a man like me to put on the clothes of a woman and to borrow her bracelets and eyelashes in order to write about her. Is it not an irony that I cry out with a woman's voice while women cannot speak out on their own."[8]

Qabbani's admiration for women did not end up with mere praise. He was genuinely concerned about emancipation of women and hence incited them to revolt against oppression by men. He says:

> Revolt, I like you to revolt
> Resist against history and gain the upper hand on the grand illusion.
> Revolt against the East which looks at you as a feast on the bed
> Don't be afraid of any one as the Sun is the graveyard of the vultures.[9]

While on one hand he appreciates the femininity and sensitivity of woman, on the other hand Qabbani encourages women and persuades them to resist the old customs and traditions of the society which imposed so many restrictions. Relying sometimes on the customs of the society and at times in the name of religion, men exploit women and explain religious teachings in the way they like. He criticizes this kind of male chauvinism bitterly in one of his poems saying:

> We spent the whole life in bedroom with an army of harem around us
> And a document of marriage in our custody
> And a deed of divorce in our hands
> And we said: Almighty has legalized (it)
> Our nights as divided (57)

Qabbani also unmasked the hypocrisy of society and the hollow manipulating of religion in his writings:

> As if the religion was a shop we had opened to satisfy ourselves.
> . . . And to enjoy the maids who are our property.
> And we twisted the word of God in the way that benefits us
> And we are not ashamed of what we do

We played with its sanctity
And its noble intent
And remembered nothing except the bed
And we took nothing from these words
Except our four wives. (63-67)

From the very beginning of his poetic career, Qabbani sided with the Arab woman and held man and the society to be responsible for the wrongs done to her. Qabbani was understanding and compassionate at all times toward women, save toward the adulteress. For her he had nothing but disdain because he viewed her as a sinner against her children since he was convinced that adultery had a destructive influence upon them.

Nizar Qabbani's stand remained essentially unchanged throughout his twenties and early thirties, which coincided with the forties and fifties of the present century (in the meantime he joined the Syrian diplomatic service after graduating from the Law School in 1945). His next four collections of poems, published during 1944 to 1950, were written in more or less the same vein. He remained obsessed by women's outer appearance and by their bodies, heedless of their inner qualities as persons. His erotic poems make the great majority of his first collections seem like one long poem in which the poet sings repetitious songs to many blurred, indistinct women. Here and there a new dimension is added to his erotic visions: nature, the moon, the clouds, rain, sparrows, even a bedroom in the city. The stage of his love poetry is wider and more delineated. One infers that Qabbani has finally graduated from theory to practice, from dreams to actual experience.

Although the majority of Qabbani's poems are either addressed to women or speak in a woman's voice, they leave the impression that these women were not specific, well-delineated persons on the whole. The underlying reason may be the general reluctance of Arab poets since pre-Islamic times to refer explicitly to their beloved lest they be recognized and disgraced (as would their tribes).' Judged by the bulk of his poems, Qabbani seems to have no particular woman in view. One also finds his love poems to be repetitive in the sense that the themes are fairly limited, while the poet's artistic talent is only deployed in the variations.

Works Cited

1. Nizār Qabbānī, "Qiṣṣati maal-Shir," *Arabian Love Poems: Full Arabic and English Texts* (Three Continents Press) Lynne Rienner, 1999, 166.
2. Nizār Qabbani, "Sayabqal Hubu sayyedi," *Ibid.*, 12.
3. Nizār Qabbānī, "Sayabqal ḥubbu Sayyedī," Beirut, Manshlūrātu Nizār Qabbānī, 2nd Edition, 1987, p: 127.
4. Nizār Qabbāni, *Arabian Love Poems*, 7.
5. Nizār Qabbānī, "Ashārun Khārijatun ala al-qānlūn," *Ibid.*, 25.
6. Nizār Qabbānī, "Qiṣṣatī maal-Shir," *Ibid.*, 132.
7. Nizār Qabbānī, "Al-amāl al-shiriyyah al-kāmilah," *Ibid.*, 86.
8. Nisar Qabbani"Yawmiyātu imraatin lā mubāliyyah," *Ibid.*, 5.
9. Nizār Qabbānī, Al-amāl al-shiriyyah al-kāmilah, *Ibid.*, 573.

In Memoriam: Bharati Mukherjee

Bharati Mukherjee (27 July 1940-28 January 2017) was an eminent Indian-American novelist and Professor Emeritus in the Department of English at the University of California, Berkeley. She made a remarkable contribution to Indian English Literature, especially Women's Studies. On her demise, Dr. Debasish Lahiri of Kolkata University paid a rich tribute to the novelist at the International Commonwealth Conference held at OUCIP, Hyderabad, in February 2017.

Editor

If the narrative of immigration is the epic narrative of this millennium, Bharati Mukherjee was its first South Asian archivist.

In many of her novels and stories, a young woman—shaped, as she was, by a patriarchal culture—strikes out for the unknown, sometimes by choice and sometimes not. In the existential crisis that ensues, a new self emerges—or a series of selves, multiple answers to the question, "Who am I?"

In *The Middleman and Other Stories* (1988), which won the National Book Critics Circle Award for fiction, Mukherjee ventriloquized the immigrant experience in the voices of newcomers from the Caribbean, the Middle East, the Philippines and Sri Lanka, all of them both daunted and intoxicated by the strange possibilities of life in the United States.

The title character and narrator of *Jasmine* (1989) is a poor Punjabi who makes her way to Florida and undergoes a series of transformations. Taking on a new identity and a new name as she moves from one job to the next, "greedy with wants and reckless from hope," she draws ever closer to the dream of shedding her old identity and achieving the American dream of self-definition.

Mukherjee evolved a credo: Make the familiar exotic—Americans would not recognize their country when she was finished with it—and make the exotic—the India of elephants and arranged marriages—familiar.

The Tiger's Daughter (1972), the most autobiographical of her works, told the story of an American-educated Indian woman who returns home to an India she no longer recognizes. She moved into less familiar territory with *Wife* (1975), taking as her main character a young Bengali woman who rebels against her arranged marriage after moving to New York.

With the story collection *Darkness* (1985), Mukherjee began to attract critical notice for her discerning portraits of immigrants struggling to cast off the bonds of tradition and remake their lives. *The Holder of the World* (1993) was a novel within a novel based in part on Hawthorne's *The Scarlet Letter*. *Desirable Daughters* (2002), which traced the different fortunes of three sisters from Calcutta, was the first in a loosely joined trilogy of novels, the others being *The Tree Bride* (2004) and *Miss New India* (2011). Throughout, the restless, hopeful surge of immigration, and the mutability of cultures, gripped her imagination. But never did it suck her into the vortex of guilt.

Mukherjee made us feel that there is a reason why the language which we inherit is called our mother tongue. It is our mother, forgiving, embracing, naming the world and all its emotions. Though she had lived for over four decades in cities in which English or French was the grist of the urban soundscape, it was Bangla that exercised motherly restraint over Mukherjee's provisional, immigrant identity. Although she had had no new thought in Bangla for half her lifetime it did not matter. As a native speaker Mukherjee had an automatic membership in what she held to be the world's most articulate, most imaginative, and most intelligent club: Bengaliness. To her inner Bengali she remained constant, as it did for her.

Simultaneous rootedness was the message of her scripting of the diaspora. The Diaspora emerged as an inspiring calm, an inviting new dawn of self-fashioning as opposed to the tempestuous and disintegrating inevitability of traditional figurations of the word. Mukherjee's vision did not cleave, it sutured. In the cold world of dispersal and loss she used the warm glue of words to keep humanity from falling away. R.I.P.

Kolkatta **Debasish Lahiri**

Creative Writing

A Himalayan Poem

An Excerpt

Nishi Chawla, an Indian-American writer, is on the faculty of Thomas Edison State University, New Jersey, U.S.A. Her fifth volume of poetry, A Himalayan Poem, *was published by Sterling in 2017. A Himalayan Poem (2017), is broken up into eight sections. The 100 page long poem is her own personal response to the landscape of the mountains even as the poem explores its physical attributes: its rivers, its peaks and glaciers, its flora and its fauna, its cultural traditions, both secular and spiritual, and its people. Section One is devoted to the origins of the Himalayas. Section Two is about the rivers and lakes found in the Himalayas. Section Three is devoted to the peaks and glaciers. Section Four is about the trees and flowers found in the Himalayas, and Section Five is about the birds and animals. Section Six is about environmental degradation. Section Seven is about temples and monasteries found in the Himalayas. The final section is about what the mountains symbolize.*

Mountain music here rises, from the dark
Eastern depths of the Tsangpo gorge, a dis-
Quieting deep, where time stands still.
Only its music ensues. Chant like, visceral.

Music that moves, soul captions of
The deepest cavern, it soars and it dips,
Uncanny laughter ensues, though there is
No straight flat line here for miles.

Mount Namche Barwe is where the

Soul explores its own lost music. Beneath
The shadow of that music, sad yet fervent,
It feels too high to touch its own shadow.

If a churning, if a music can be created out
Of a collision, pulsing and surging between
Two tectonic plates, crush and break into
A fifteen hundred mile long mountain arc.

NISHI CHAWLA (U.S.A.)

Students have to be involved!

If you treat students like retards—
they will become retarded!

In the classroom—
the teacher dominates;
and students become fixtures. . .
like the furniture—
tables, chairs.
Mute, unresponsive,
they gradually tune off, doze.

The teacher notices,
but pretends not to care so much.
But, after a while, he works up his mind
when he finds he has mustered enough courage
and starts slamming them down.
He shouts, yells, even tries to humiliate.

Is he building up students
as he is supposed to—

or is he making them shrink
into their shells?

Is there much learning taking place
in his classroom?

Oughtn't a facilitator ensure
that learning happens?

Oughtn't students be involved!

If only the self-styled educator
would stop presuming
he knew it all
and recognised the infinite potential
of the young minds in front of him!

Listen!
Be a catalyst!
Stimulate active thinking!

Education ought to be an experience!
Help cultivate interest in things around
and develop application-oriented thinking!

Let the classroom come alive!

BENISON (K.L. University, Guntur)

The 'Court'ship Rite

A poignant critique of the painted legal and judiciary system in verse!
Editor

Look beyond the painted mural
Masquerading legal arsenal

Savour the wit and the ire
Clothed in black and white attire

Maintain protocol and hierarchy
Amidst order and anarchy

Pass for or pass it over
Intrigued strategies, the legal flavour

Justice delayed or justice denied
Brunt of patience perseverance to abide

Appealing appalling or benumbed sight
The eternal saga, the 'court'ship rite

Sumita Puri (Dyal Singh (E) College, University of Delhi)

Strange are the Ways of the Lord

ROSWITHA JOSHI

The story by the eminent Indo-German writer Roswitha Joshi reminds us of the first lines of a poem by Goethe. In the author's translation, they read 'Why to move into the distance, when the good things lie so near?" It is a slightly fictionalized account of a personal ATM experience made and written about before (!) the advent of demonetization and the upheaval it caused.

Editor

Her husband had left in a hurry, just thrown a few things in his travel bag and then dashed towards the door, his wiry body thrown forward like that of a sprinter who wanted to stick his nose first over the finishing line. His head was fast balding, his cheeks sunken. They were also flushed. Frown lines and dark under-eye patches made him look older than his 45 years. The competition was stiff. He feared that a major contract would be cancelled. Recently he had said 'fuck' and 'shit' more often than usual, and that was a bad sign.

"Where are you going?" she asked.

"Airport. Emergency meeting. Fire fighting."

"Where?"

"Frankfurt."

"What happened?"

His lips quivered. His hands shook. He waved them impatiently at no one in particular before banging the door shut. He gave her neither an answer nor the chance to ask for anything, money included.

Standing at the window, she watched him twisting his body into a taxi and then wipe his brow. She followed the car with her eyes, the way it snaked through the unruly traffic, shrunk into a white dot and disappeared in the two- and four-wheeled horde of office goers. He would reach the airport just in time, as usual, she mused pressing her nose against the glass pane.

She too was worried, though on a comparatively minor scale. She had to pay an electricity bill that had skipped her attention, and today was the last day before the supply would be cut and she deprived of comforts like cool air and hot food, not to mention the light needed for doing what she fancied to do.

The rooms were dark, shaded by small canopies above the windows to keep the glare out. Their home had been built when the desire for indoor brightness was not yet there and air-conditioning a distant dream. They had bought it because it was cozy and compact without an inch of wasted space, unlike so many places they had gone to see.

The electricity bill amounted to about 10,000 Rupees. Had she not bought that stylish silk shirt yesterday, she would have had enough cash. Now her purse was empty and her cupboard fuller than ever. Smiling at her self-indulgence, she was sure that a walk to the local ATM machine would solve the problem and, whistling a popular tune, leisurely ambled over to the small market around the corner.

The ATM booth was occupied and remained so for quite a while. Whipping on her feet, she impatiently watched a young man in a leather jacket insert his card, retrieve it and insert it again and again. She also saw him hammering against the machine and then abruptly turn around, his face a grimace of fury and frustration.

"Is the machine not working?" she asked.

"Try it yourself," he grumbled, before roaring off on his Enfield.

Maybe the guy's card did not work because it was scratched, she thought and, confidently, pushed her smooth one into the slot. She equally confidently keyed in the code number and amount desired. Yet, her first attempt failed, and so did her second and third one. "Damn it," she shrugged and dropped the card back into her purse.

I will try another machine, after all, Delhi is full of them, she consoled herself and hurried home to pick up her car keys. She then drove off to a bigger market where several ATM machines stood their ground. She went to the nearest one. Two mechanics squatted inside the booth with their toolbox wide open. When she knocked at the door, they grinned as wide as their toolbox was open and pointed at a sheet of paper they had stuck to the glass. It read: Machine out of order.

"Can't you read," one of them grumbled, while the other feasted his eyes on her legs.

"F. . .," she stopped herself and, keeping her lips zipped, walked back to her car to drive to the other side of the market, where she had espied another machine encased in its glass and metal box. A woman resembling the dog she carried stepped out and, shaking her head, mumbled, "There seems to be no money in that bloody tin box."

"Gosh. Do you know of another machine here?" she asked, frowning.

"Yes, but none of them works. I tried them all."

Not one to easily give up, she drove to a market further away to try her luck. The cubicle housing the ATM machine there was empty, yet when she pushed the door, it did not yield an inch. It was locked.

Meanwhile, not only her mood had darkened but the sky too. Grey clouds floated towards each other. Soon they would gather above her head into a black sieve dispensing streams of water. She decided to call it quits and drive home before the roads got flooded.

Alone at home and that too with an empty purse, she did what homemakers do when they have nothing better to do: she rummaged in a cupboard to rearrange things that she had already rearranged about a hundred times. Yet, only recently had she detected, deeply buried in herself, the generosity to discard items she had not used for years but found too good to be given away. Today she would weed out the chaff from the wheat to make room for new stuff. Nowadays, there were such beautiful quilts and sheets in the market, she sighed, and would have gone shopping straight away, if only she had the means.

Wearily, she opened the linen cupboard and pulled out piles of sheets and pillowcases. When she was about to inspect them piece by piece a bundle fell out. She picked it up and could not believe her eyes. The bundle consisted of several packs of hundred rupee notes, stapled and then tied together with a rubber band. Like Dabogert Duck, she counted and realized that she was holding exactly the ten thousand rupees she had tried to extract from the ATM machines. Had a benign God come to her rescue, she wondered though she had called herself an atheist—so far.

Only later did she come to know that the benign God was her husband, who had, years ago, quickly deposited the bundle between the sheets, when a courier boy relentlessly rung the bell and delivered a letter that deeply disturbed him. In fact, it disturbed him so much that he forgot all about the money.

The Icicles of Eggertsville

HOWARD R. WOLF
Amherst, NY

Ernest Hemingway's "The Snows of Kilimanjaro" serves as the background of "The Icicles of Eggertsville." The ironic contrast between the protagonists both enlarges and diminishes Ludwig's loss of a romantic partner. He is a comic, but enlightened, loser. Given the brevity of the genre, short fiction benefits from allusive echoes. The author met Hemingway at the Ritz Hotel, Paris, in 1956.

Editor

It had begun quietly, but quickly, in mid-January among noisy teenagers giggling over selfies at Starbucks and ended decisively in an awkward and painful exit a year later. Nine months had passed since he had fallen again from what he had hoped would be a peak romantic experience? What had happened?

During the long Buffalo winters, when icicles the length of cathedral organ pipes hung like stalactites on the eaves of his small house (*eaves of glass*, he smirked to himself), he had tried to figure out why life had served up loss as a favorite dish to him. Or, perhaps, he had prepared it in ways that he didn't understand. Maybe it just was a delayed birth trauma or a universal constant.

He just needed to face unpleasant facts and tell himself the truth, never easy for anyone, and since truth was rooted in the loam of childhood, maybe there was no out of the thicket of his aloneness, the momentary nausea of abandonment. No matter, he wasn't about to turn in his introspective trowel.

He was in the twilight of his life, but twilight lingered during the summers in Western New York as a reprieve after what felt like a winter in a valley below Mt. Everest. These long twilights, even now on a mellow late October evening, with a breeze stirring the lower branches of his blue spruce, gave him hope that there was some positive motion in the world left for him.

And now that he had a small deck where he could perch, as if he were on watch in the crow's nest of a New Bedford whaler, he could hear the rich at play who lived beyond the blue spruce and over a chain-fence and imagine that some life-enhancing days lay ahead.

Hemingway loved the words "beyond" and "over." They created a space for the mind to hunt in. Ludwig was no Hem, but he loved the old man's arrow-pointed words, and once as an act of homage he had laid a pine branch on papa's grave in Ketchum, Idaho.

He would reread some of the old man's stories and see if they could help him get beyond and over a recent emotional wound, the *cojones* of the heart. Now older than the old man when he ended his pain, Ludwig still looked to him, perhaps foolishly, for guidance.

How he had managed to end up . . . he searched for the right and true words . . . *alone on his deck*? How had he managed to watch icicles as big as the Ritz lengthen during the long winter nights of Eggertsville, New York, a suburb of Buffalo, without an empathetic companion by his side to soothe his aching limbs and spirits? What had he done to make Rita, his senorita from Malibu, cut the cord six months ago that bound them umbilically together, or so he had thought?

The story of his failure, hers, theirs, everyone's, was worth a book in itself. It was a job for a poet, and though Ludwig was an ex-bard, he still would give it the old college try, as they used to say in the pre-Viet Nam era before a new generation had said kaddish for the Ivy League's rah-rah spirit.

But the writer's muse could be a real bitch, especially the Israeli beauty, Delilah, a visiting assistant professor of Diasporic Studies, who had left him in a ditch decades ago when she hooked up with an editor at *The Daily Forward* after he had accepted one of her articles, "Shrunken Lives in the American Diaspora." She certainly had cut Ludwig down to size in more than one way. For years he even had checked his dingle when he woke up to make sure it was still dangling, but he had soldiered on.

Now, wounded again, he would try to make sense of the past and then write about all the places he and Rita had planned to see together and where they were when they made their plans, a future that never would become their present.

Their future had quickly become a ruin in the past like the Catskill resort of his adolescence when he had worked as a boat-boy at Scaroon Manor on Schroon Lake, an upper notch on the Borscht Belt in the lower Adirondacks.

If the timbers of the faux log cabins of Grossinger's the Concord, and Scaroon Manor could be repurposed as planks for Hasidic Sukkot huts, it might be possible for Ludwig the self-inquisitor to put himself on trial in an effort to salvage some splinters and spars from his recent land-locked shipwreck.

If he was mixing metaphors, not highballs, he chortled, it only made sense because he had been balled-up for most of his life. If his psyche was Grand Central Station, few trains ever reached Greenwich without being derailed.

How did their end begin? What did he know and when did he know it? *It's Watergate all over again*, he guffawed mutedly, but he now had a special opportunity to find out why and how he-she-they had come to an end. And he was ready to examine the past as he sat on his deck, a glass of kosher *Lower Golan Prosecco* in one hand, an OptiFlow pen, *his* 6.5 Mannlicher, in the other.

The Yellow taxi to take him to the Buffalo airport for his flight to JFK and then El Al to Tel Aviv, where his faraway daughter lived, wouldn't come until 6:30 a.m., and he was packed, socks rolled like bullets in the chambers of a six-shooter. He had all night to weave together the torn fabric of the past like the shawl he had bought for Rita at Tel Aviv's Carmel Market, not knowing that it was rent goods. The cab might be Yellow, but Ludwig would face the charging bull of the past with a graceful Veronica like Juan Belmonte.

He wasn't sure it could be stitched together. No tailor, like his grandfather, no garment centre manufacturer like his father, Ludwig nonetheless had inherited some of the instincts of the needle trades. At the end of the day, words and phrases weren't so different from swatches and end-pieces. Something could be made of them if you weren't into bespoke tailoring like Henry James or Prince Charles.

As his father had shipped women's coats to Sears and J.C. Penny, so Ludwig had written fiction for women's magazines, an occasional essay on cultural fashion in *Women's Wear Daily*, and a few articles on the "lost" American writers of the 1920s, enough to get him tenure at a small college on the outskirts of Buffalo, but not enough to retire as a Full professor.

Well, he had made a life and things began to look up when Rita tripped at Starbuck's that winter afternoon and he had caught her Smart-Phone. She couldn't have been more grateful if he were Sir Lancelot and had returned her green scarf, so she invited him to chat over a café au lait.

She knew more about social media than he did about Shakespeare. It was easy for him, at a loss in the electronic world, to ask questions, and she, a Quaker-Buddhist-social worker, was impressed by how selfless he seemed to be, how eager he was to learn. She knew he was chatting her up and hitting on her, but she liked the style of his pitch. You could judge a man by the quality of his come-on, and she had been alone for too long with her thoughts of the tragic mystery in her life.

They texted one another for a week in which he picked out his wit and she said that the wattage of her inner light had glowed somewhat more brightly since the meeting at Starbuck's had brought them together.

The word "somewhat" stung, but he had repressed its bite.

Both adults, she sixty, he, seventy, it then only had taken them a one day-trip a week later to a winery along the southern shore of Lake Ontario for them to get together under the Amish quilts in her spacious country house on the outskirts of Buffalo where the deer roamed, an 1880s farmhouse that reminded him of the cottage in Austria where Hemingway had written *The Sun Also Rises*. Maybe Rita, comely and stylish, could be his elder Hadley.

They seemed quickly to fit. She liked clever men. Her late husband Cliff, an MIA of sorts, had been an astrophysicist, mountain climber, and a Los Angeles County champion Scrabble player, and when Ludwig said he "preferred quilts to guilt," she had been charmed.

"I think we might have a lot to talk about," she said,

"I like to find nice spots for conversations. Do you know Golden Hill State Park? It's empty this time of year. There's even a lighthouse there."

That "might" should have made him wary, but he wanted to get closer to her and half-believed he could woo her away from the past with words. He would try to fit into her life, even if it meant, with his L-5 stenosis, limping along the shores of Lake Ontario. He would try to walk the walk and talk the talk so he could get to the underwater floor of a relationship with her.

If Freud had taught his generation anything, it was that you had to become a deep-sea diver to get to the bottom of a relationship. Ludwig doubted if Freud had ever gone into the water above his waist, or bungee-jumped into the Rhine, but he had saved many drowning psyches through the CPR of insight.

"I'll try to go with you to as many places as possible," he said, without adding that he'd be limping most of the time. "Towards" and "trying" were key words for Ludwig, and many of his amatory exes, more than filled a tic-tac toe box, had found his quest for a shared seabed to be a lead-sinker.

"Too needy" had been the pink slip and discarded negligee at the end of more than a few trysts, especially with the women who were themselves questing souls, who didn't want to be tethered to a man's dependency. And Rita had made it clear that first night that she was searching for a "summit beyond suffering, an eternal present."

She liked having him in her bed with winter deepening, but she wanted to be alone, finally, where she depended on no one and no one clung to her.

"Good," she said, "we can make a list of all the places we'd like to see together. It can be our game."

They would have had a better chance of making it together, he now realized, if they had been Canadian geese, paired for life, inconsolable at separation, but he had taken the plunge that night with only a moment's hesitation. And they really did seem to fit. It was, he whispered to her, after their first caress, *as if two missing adjoining pieces of a jigsaw puzzle had turned up.* A lover of board games, she was delighted by the image.

"Cliff loved board games before," she hesitated, "but he disappeared."

"Disappeared?" he asked, gently.

"Sort of" she said, "he went missing at Mount Saraswati ten years ago, the Indian Astronomical Observatory in the Himalayas, highest one in the world."

"I'm sorry," he said.

She didn't say anything at first, but snuggled more tightly, as if the crevice between them needed to be closed.

"I'm trying to get over it, it's difficult, we had no children, he didn't think he could be a strong enough father. His childhood had been too painful, his father was a suicide, a twin brother alcoholic. He lived with a deep hole in his soul, we just had each other. I tried to fill it, but I never could be sure if I was as giving as I needed to be," she said, barely audible, and became silent.

"But he was doing what he needed to do," she continued. "He went to the highest places to test his resources, to find out if he was strong enough, but something went wrong. They're still looking for him on the north face of the mountain. He seemed to be walking in that direction. "

"I'm sorry again. I know about searching," he said, "I've been seeing a shrink for years, spelunking in the unconscious."

"And he was a great Scrabble player," she said, pressing closer, "I used to love the game, but after Cliff disappeared, I began to meditate. I needed to find a place in the universe where I belong, just me. Aren't we made of the same particles? The universe is still a mystery."

"Like the brain," he said, trying to bring her closer, "it seems to be as complicated as the universe."

If she looked to Carl Sagan for meaning, he had found more, at least in his youth, in Francois Sagan, but he buttoned his lip. After all, he had learned something about buttons in the garment centre from his father, a Seventh Avenue *shmatte* merchant, whose father had sold "old clothes" off a pushcart on Canal Street.

"I keep searching for that inner Shangri-la. I mediate every morning at dawn. I keep searching for the right mantra, the one that will put me in touch with the music of the spheres. Sometimes I hum and chant, listening for the right harmony."

"I should go home then and let you sleep."

"No, you can sleep in as long as you want, it's a weekend, I'll have breakfast when you wake up. I'm glad you're here. It helps. I need to move on."

Looking back, he knew he should have left at that point. She wasn't likely to find him in a movie version of *Lost Horizon*. He was no Ronald Coleman. But if they spent enough time together in all the places they both wanted to see in which they could learn more about each other, he hoped that she could accept him fully.

He thought of Pascal. If Rita could give up her quest for the "infinitely large," she might accept him as the "infinitely small," but no *schlemiel*. If he couldn't be an Adirondack peak, he was, at least, Mt. Murray where he had worked as a boat-boy one summer in the upper Catskills.

And they fit together so tightly and gracefully that leaving would have felt like emotional hara-kiri. She felt that, too, at least at first, he had hoped. "Look," she said, their entwined arms casting a shadow on the oak panels of her bedroom, "we could be mistaken for strands of kelp."

"Maybe we can kelp each other."

"I hope so," she said, laughing and then curved the arch of her foot against his leg, "see, we're like two shells, one resting in the other, a coral reef."

He wanted at that time to think that they might meet in the deep sea vents of a late middle age relationship, an Indian summer of sorts. After all, they were partners in loss, she as the result of a tragic enigma and he, long divorced after a traumatic betrayal, the father of an only child who had decided to make a new life in Israel.

"We can visit some of the places that inspired me," he said, matching his fingers with Rita's, "and you can show me some of the landscapes that lifted your spirits. We'll learn from each other."

"For example?"

"Mt. Rushmore."

"Not until they carve the face of a woman president," she said.

"And you?"

"San Miguel de Allende."

"Mexico?" he asked.

"Yes, my father took us there after the war. He wanted to write a novel about his traumatic experience, the men who were lost in his bomber squadron. You could live on the cheap there, and he had the G.I. Bill. Your turn."

"Don't rush, I don't want to use up all my geographical tiles. Which reminds me, I can show you the Byzantine mosaics at Tsiporri."

"Where is that?"

"Israel, it's like the seven layers of Troy."

"One more, please, I like this game."

"How about Cascais?"

"Where in Emerson's name is that?"

"Emerson?"

"I'm part Unitarian," she said, "but where's Cascais?"

"On the Tagus River, ten miles from Lisbon, where the estuary meets the sea. I saw it when I took a year off from college and backpacked across Europe. I'd like to show you some of the places that I'd still like to write about and the things that happened there."

"Tell me more."

"Just one more. Key West, you'd like that, Hemingway lived there. The Israeli bitch and I had the 'good destruction' there before she totalled me, and I ended up in Hemingway's collision shop. Eventually, we can go to Cuba and see Finca Vigia where he lived like a lion king. The country's bound to open up one of these days. But you really need to sleep."

"You're right," she said, turning away slightly, but pulling his arm around her waist as if she were a mountain climber and needed a safety line. He was pleased to be one, at least for a while, if that's what she needed him to be.

And as a harvest moon, as vivid as an Ansel Adams photograph, cast a glow over them, he thought of Kim Novak and William Holden dancing to the tune of "Moonglow" in *Picnic*. He and Rita weren't as young and attractive, but he was something of a drifter, and *they had come together as lonely strangers* at Starbucks, the subject of his only published article, "Shared Isolation in America: Communion at Twilight" (*Jesuitical and Talmudic Studies*, Spring 1976), but it had gotten him his tenure and made a small dent in the fender of the academic world.

As he drifted into sleep, he dreamed about what he came to call his billiard ball theory of anxiety, his only attempt at a scientific model of experience. Each large Daliesque ball represented, as he came to decipher it later, a romantic avalanche in which he had been buried. As he was about to run out of air to breathe, another ball rolled along and knocked the first one into a pocket, just as Rita seemed to be someone who might knock the memory of Delilah off the green felt.

As winter lengthened and they played more place-games with each other after uncertain love-making, uncertain that she was letting him deeply into her life, he began to gain a measure of confidence that he and Rita were a couple who had rescued each other from solitude.

But he wasn't sure that she had found the inner harmony that would make that possible. It occurred to him one night that it might make a good board-game. Each question could be a card that might land them on *TOO ALONE TO FAIL.*

"What place would you most like us to see together?" he asked one night.

"That's a tough one, maybe Lantau Island, just a few miles from Hong Kong in the South China Sea. There's a Buddhist temple at the top of small mountain. My father said he had found some peace there after the war."

"And you, what would you most like us to see together?"

"Talk about tough. Maybe Terengganu, an island off the East Coast of Malaysia. I went snorkelling there one moonlit night along a coral reef. I never felt so connected to life, sounds lame, I know, but I don't know how else to say it. Or maybe Mt. Hermon in Israel. You can see Lebanon and Syria from its upper ridges. It all looks like one peaceful land at that height. One snowfall is general over all the region, a one world solution."

"Herman?"

"No, he lives in the Bronx, Her*mon*, Israel's only snow-capped peak."

"Connection is everything," she said as she eased into sleep.

When she slipped out of bed at dawn, he pretended still to be asleep, but he wanted to find out if her meditation was helping her get closer to the place where she wanted to be. Her breathing and humming, her words, if audible, might be a key.

He would be a spy in the camp of her inner life.

He waited a few minutes and tip-toed towards her meditation room at the top of the stairs. She kept her back to the slightly open door, so she didn't notice him peering in. She sat cross-legged in front of a small statue of the Buddha, rosy cheeked children clinging to him, at whose sides two joss sticks glowed slightly in the predawn light. A sandal-wood framed photograph was placed evenly above the porcelain statue. Ludwig listened carefully, but couldn't make out any of the words.

She seemed to be murmuring something haltingly, but it might have been only uneven breathing, and he couldn't make out the figure in the faintly visible photograph who seemed to be standing on a snow-capped mountain. Or maybe it was the Taj Mahal. He couldn't be sure. Something white seemed to be gleaming.

He leaned toward the opening in the door and held his own breath so he could make out more clearly what she was saying, if she was uttering words. In the quiet of his inner ear, he thought he heard her weeping as she looked up at the photograph and extended her arms in what seemed to be a beckoning and welcoming gesture, like Gatsby staring at the green light.

He thought of the lonely times after Delilah had pink-slipped him when he had stood at the end of Anglin's Pier in Lauderdale-by-the-Sea during the period of his visits to his parents in the years of their exile in Florida. Watching Princess Line cruise ships ease their way out of Port Everglades as they headed towards the Caribbean, he had felt stuck at the red traffic light of his life. But, then, so many years later, Rita tripped at Starbucks, and he began to believe that they might become a two-person navy and see the world together.

Not to be, he thought, as her weeping became somewhat more audible, *I can't fill the gap in her life, we'll never travel together, I'll never see those places that I wanted to write about.*

Goodbye, Vasco de Gama, hello, Prince Irving the Navigator of the inner map.

There was no way to pre-shrink hope, and he had gone for the bait again like a fish suckered by a lure. He had seen many tropical fish lose their iridescence in a flash when they were hooked and left flapping on Anglin's pier. Ludwig remembered Hemingway's dismissive description of Dos Passos: "White as the under half of an unsold flounder at 11 o'clock in the morning."

Still, he felt a surge of empathy for Rita in this moment, and as he began to step into her room to comfort her, she, sensing him, turned around suddenly.

"You should be sleeping, not invading my space," she almost shouted.

Embarrassed, at a loss for words, and reduced to a stammer, he stepped quickly back and found himself sliding down the carpeted staircase whose thick nap cushioned his descent. Panicked that he might not live to add another publication to his slim bibliography, he managed to protect his head by rolling himself somehow into a ball as if he were a pink *Spaldeen* from the schoolyard of his New York City childhood and bounced into the laundry basket that Rita had put at the bottom of the staircase before they went to bed.

"Oh, my god, oh, my god," he heard her scream as he was engulfed in sheets that bore the scent of their love-making. She rushed down the stairs and did her best to pull him out of the snowfield of white linen in which he seemed to be buried.

"It's okay," he said, "I think I can stand."

"I thought I had lost you, I wasn't sure I'd be able to talk to you again."

"It's okay, I don't think I broke anything. I didn't lose my footing on Kilimanjaro."

She reached out to help him up.

"I can't forget what might have happened," she said almost inaudibly.

"I know," he said, after a long pause, I've known it for some time, but I kept hoping."

"We can still travel together, you can still write about what we see together," she said as she wrapped her arms around him protectively.

"I appreciate that, we'll see what we can work out, it may take some time."

"You make us some coffee, I'll finish my meditation and join you."

Those were the last words they exchanged.

He managed to get upstairs to dress and then to descend quietly without disturbing her inner journey to get to a higher place beyond suffering.

***

A MASH Urgent Care Ambulance stopped at the house across the street where the recluse lived. Ludwig had tried to befriend him from time to time, but it had been hopeless. He always knew that this was the way life would end for the "lonely guy," as the kids on the street called him. He never returned. The house was sold to a couple from Northern India.

The flashing lights of the ambulance snapped Ludwig out of his deep rumination. He checked his watch—3 a.m. The taxi would come in a few hours to take him to the airport. He needed to get some sleep if he didn't want to look like a survivor of the Titanic when he arrived in Israel.

He would show Rita. He was determined to see and write about the places they had named as they played their night-games, places she wouldn't see now. *I may have fallen into the laundry basket*, he thought, *and I might be a loser, but I'm not defeated.*

She had squeezed the globe of his future into a ball, to say nothing about his *cojones*, but he would bounce back. He was wounded, but not broken. He hoped Hem was right: "The world breaks every one and afterward many are strong in the broken places."

Maybe my loss has been a gain, an itinerary and motive to travel, he thought. Diminished, but somehow expanded, he would keep going somewhere east of Suez after Israel. If he got to India, he might go to that observatory to see if he could find out what had happened to Rita's lost husband.

He might be able to find out something that would help Rita rise above her suffering. Maybe her husband had left a loving note for her etched in an ice-field, something to let her know that she had never let him down, no matter what had caused his disappearance. If he could find out something helpful, Rita might reach out to him again.

If nothing else, it would give Ludwig something to write about. That would be his safety net. It always had been the place where he could make a gain out of a loss in life's balance sheet and kick a few field goals like Fitzgerald's Princeton football hero, Hobey Baker, even if he lost the game.

So long as he believed in his writing, he would be ok. That had been difficult sometimes, especially in the beginning of his self-imprisonment in the Halls of Poison Ivy when colleagues acted more like lifetime members in Freud's primal hoard than fellow spelunkers in Plato's cave who were groping in common for the truth.

Well, he was on the move. He didn't want Rita to think that she had pushed him down the stairs. He would send her upbeat postcards as he made his way along, he chortled, the *gabardine road* of his life. And who knew? Maybe she would give up mourning and show up one dawn at the old Moulmein pagoda or wherever he might be.

Enough day-dreaming. It was time to leave. It would feel like a lifetime before the taxi came, but it would come. It always had come on time before, and there was no reason why it wouldn't come on time this time. It had been and still might be a good company.